A PRACTICAL GUIDE TO CONCRETE PAVEMENT TECHNOLOGY FOR DEVELOPING COUNTRIES

DECEMBER 2021

ASIAN DEVELOPMENT BANK

Contents

Tables and Figures

TABLES

FIGURES

Foreword

Durability and reliability are key characteristics that a developing country's transportation system must possess. Quality of infrastructure must be ensured to enable unhampered economic activities that will help a nation to attain its socioeconomic goals. Hence, planning and construction of infrastructure like road networks must be pursued with deliberate partiality toward economic viability, social acceptability, and environmental sustainability.

It is from this perspective that I am pleased to present to the various transport sector stakeholders of the Asian Development Bank (ADB) this pioneering guide on concrete pavement technology.

This guide was prepared by a team composed of Pawan Karki, senior transport specialist, along with CWRD colleagues in the Uzbekistan Resident Mission and ADB headquarters in Manila, officials from the Government of Uzbekistan, and consultant Michel DiTommaso. This was undertaken with generous support from the People's Republic of China Poverty Reduction and Regional Cooperation Fund and the Republic of Korea e-Asia and Knowledge Partnership Fund.

Anchored in the experiences of transport sector projects of countries in Asia and the Pacific, this guide aims to support transport sector executing agencies in the planning and implementation of concrete pavement construction projects. It specifically addresses a defined need—the lack, among transport executing agencies in the region, of sufficient experience in the design and construction of concrete pavements. This weakness results in poorly planned, constructed, and maintained concrete road networks.

This guide provides transport sector stakeholders key technical information to enhance their understanding of issues and concerns relating to planning, designing, constructing, and maintaining concrete roads. Written in simple language, the material is replete with practical examples from case studies and existing literature on the subject.

Concrete roads have been proven to be durable and safe, enabling unimpeded flow of people, goods, and services over longer periods of time. Efficient travel reduces carbon emissions, resulting in positive contribution toward the attainment of the Sustainable Development Goals.

On behalf of CWRD's Transport and Communications Division family, I proudly share with you
A Practical Guide to Concrete Pavement Technology for Developing Countries.

Hideaki Iwasaki
Director
Transport and Communications Division
Central and West Asia Department
Asian Development Bank

Purpose of the Guide

Many countries are exploring the use of concrete pavements to improve the reliability of their road networks. However, executing agencies do not yet have sufficient experience designing and constructing concrete pavements. This can lead to problems such as the need for premature and costly repairs or maintenance.

This publication aims to provide key technical information to asset managers, clients, designers, and contractors, as a guide to planning, designing, and constructing concrete roads. It provides a basis for understanding the behavior of jointed plain concrete pavements (JPCP) and how to maximize their properties while keeping the risk of defective work at a minimum.

JPCPs are the most common type of pavement for roads and highways and the required service life is achieved through proper thickness; sufficient flexural strength; and by placing, compacting, texturing, and curing durable concrete capable of resisting the surface wear exerted by traffic. They are preferred to continuously reinforced concrete pavements because of the ease of installation and because they are easy to repair or replace unlike reinforced concrete slabs.

Basic knowledge of the main factors that affect the performance of concrete pavements is required to weigh the risks and outcomes of specific design, construction, and material-related choices.

This guide provides practical examples gathered from real case studies. It is the result of a combination of selected international literature on the topic and real-life examples collected on concrete pavements around the world. It is the first in a series focusing on specific topics for concrete pavements (life-cycle cost analysis and maintenance, road geotechnics, quality control of materials, etc.). This guide on concrete pavement technology primarily deals with the following:

Strains, stresses, and design of concrete pavements. The guide gives an overview of the types of strains and stresses building up in concrete pavements as a consequence of the environment, material properties, and external loads. Some methods from literature in English and some examples of mechanistic design are given as well to provide the reader with the theoretical tools to evaluate how the varying boundary conditions may influence the magnitude of stresses in the pavement.

Influence of aggregates on concrete pavements performance. It provides a comprehensive overview on how aggregate properties influence fresh concrete properties, as well as the strength and durability of concrete pavements. Aggregates make up to 80% of the concrete volume and they play a major role in concrete pavement performance. Many of the issues related to failing concrete pavements can be related to the use of defective aggregates. In this section, some rules for proportioning aggregates specifically for concrete pavements are also introduced.

Production of concrete for rigid pavements. It deals with the workability of concrete and how to achieve a desired rheology for the fresh mix using admixtures (plasticizers, superplasticizers, retarders). The influence of porosity, absorption, and the volume of voids on some key properties of concrete are discussed, as well as the performance of air-entraining admixtures. The control of moisture content of aggregates and the do's and don'ts in stockpiles management at batching plants is emphasized. The influence of the component temperature on the fresh concrete temperature is thoroughly discussed, along with an overview of the main parts of a modern batching plant.

Management of stress relief joints. The guide covers the critical points to be considered when designing and building contraction, construction, and expansion joints, which are among the most important features for the performance of pavements.

Curing of concrete pavements. It covers the benefits of curing, types of curing, and the planning of curing.

Common defects in concrete pavements. Discusses and presents real-life examples of the typical defects encountered in concrete pavements both as defective work observed during construction and/or as long-term distresses in service.

There are technical, economic, and social reasons to consider concrete pavements as a viable alternative to asphalt pavements in certain countries.

The main **technical reason** for preferring concrete to asphalt is the ability of concrete to resist external loads and deformations year-round. Ordinary bitumen will rut with low traffic speed (queuing trucks for instance) and rutting will be exacerbated by heat (summer). The same bitumen may crack in winter under thermal cycles acting on the pavement. The combined result is a reduced service life of the pavement. Although Superpave technology has successfully introduced new types of bitumen capable of resisting heavy loads at high and low temperature, the production and stability of such bitumen requires skilled manufacturers and users who might not be available.

Moreover, quality control of Superpave materials requires a well-equipped, advanced, and expensive laboratory. As an example, a single piece of equipment (rheometer), used to provide the classification of Superpave bitumen in terms of viscosity and complex modulus for quality control purposes, may cost as much as a fully equipped laboratory to test the basic properties of concrete all together. On the other hand, good quality concrete mixes can be designed and produced in most contexts, as long as some basic rules applicable for all types of concrete mixes (with some extra rules specific for concrete for pavements) are followed. Testing of concrete materials is also generally easier and cheaper to handle.

Economic reasons to favor concrete include maintenance costs and use of locally available materials. Although building concrete pavements may have an initial higher cost than asphalt pavements, well designed and well-built concrete pavements may last twice as long as asphalt pavements (30–40 years versus 15–20 years), provided that ordinary maintenance is done to joints and surface texture. Hence, the overall life-cycle cost to asset managers of a well-built concrete pavement is lower than for an asphalt pavement. Also, in places where bitumen must be imported and cement is locally available, consuming cement helps local economies versus expensive imports of raw materials.

Finally, from a **social perspective**, in countries with a high rate of unemployment, the use of people in labor-intensive technologies, such as concrete paving, may help increase job opportunities for workers.

It is important to limit initial defective work in concrete pavements to ensure that the long-term technical and economic benefits are fully exploited by asset managers. The aim of this guide is to provide inputs and some food for thought to help users appreciate the subtle boundary between good and bad work, and the important variables to be considered from design to execution, including production of concrete and concrete pavement.

Abbreviations

ASR	alkali-silca reaction
ASTM	American Society for Testing and Materials
CF	coarseness factor
CTE	coefficient of thermal expansion
EN	European standard
FM	fineness modulus
JPCP	jointed plain concrete pavements
LTE	load transfer efficiency
SR	stress ratio
SSD	saturated-surface-dry

1

Jointed Plain Concrete Pavements— Volumetric Stability and Design

A. Introduction and Overview

Jointed plain concrete pavements (JPCP) are the most common type of pavements for roads, highways, and airports. They mainly rely on thickness and support from a stiff foundation to perform in service.

For highways, the shape of the pavement is such that the longitudinal direction (x – direction, or length) is many orders of magnitude larger than the transversal direction (y – direction, or width) (Figure 1). The longitudinal direction is sometimes called the "paving direction," from the methodology of placing concrete using concrete pavers (Figure 2).

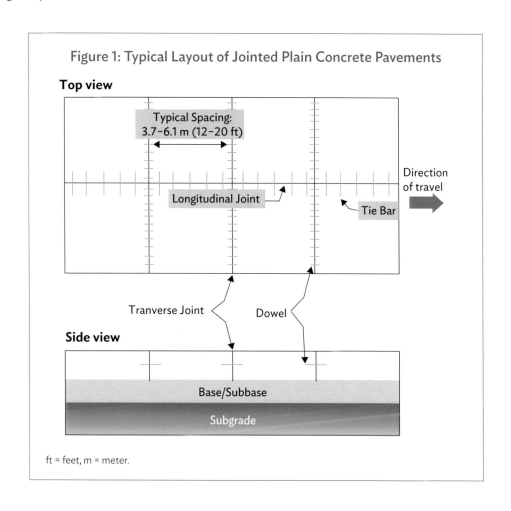

Figure 1: Typical Layout of Jointed Plain Concrete Pavements

Top view

Typical Spacing:
3.7–6.1 m (12–20 ft)

Direction of travel

Longitudinal Joint

Tie Bar

Tranverse Joint

Dowel

Side view

Base/Subbase

Subgrade

ft = feet, m = meter.

Concrete pavement. A 5.0-meter wide newly paved airfield concrete strip 0.5-meter thick.

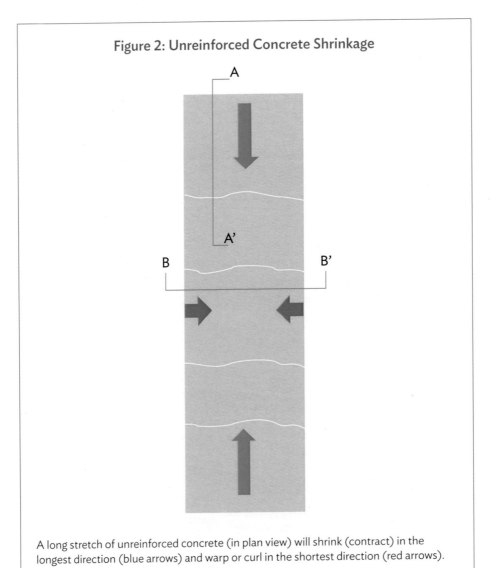

Figure 2: Unreinforced Concrete Shrinkage

A long stretch of unreinforced concrete (in plan view) will shrink (contract) in the longest direction (blue arrows) and warp or curl in the shortest direction (red arrows).

The main advantage of JPCP is that production is quicker and repair or removal is simpler compared to continuously reinforced concrete pavements, which are pavements where steel reinforcement is used to control cracking.

There is a common saying among professionals involved in concrete paving that *"a poorly designed but well-constructed pavement will last longer than a well-designed but poorly constructed one."*

While the design process is a straightforward operation depending on the skills and experience of the designer, construction combines factors of influence from several sources—production, delivery, placing, compacting, curing, and repairs. Many more things can go wrong during construction than during design.

B. Dimensional Stability

When a long strip of non-reinforced concrete is laid, it will shrink in the longest direction and it will warp or curl in the shortest direction (Figures 3 and 4).

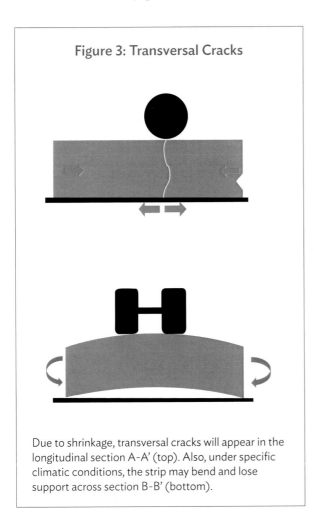

Figure 3: Transversal Cracks

Due to shrinkage, transversal cracks will appear in the longitudinal section A-A' (top). Also, under specific climatic conditions, the strip may bend and lose support across section B-B' (bottom).

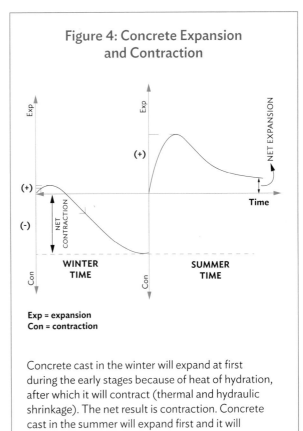

Figure 4: Concrete Expansion and Contraction

Exp = expansion
Con = contraction

Concrete cast in the winter will expand at first during the early stages because of heat of hydration, after which it will contract (thermal and hydraulic shrinkage). The net result is contraction. Concrete cast in the summer will expand first and it will contract afterward. The net result is expansion, because the magnitude of contraction is lower than the magnitude of expansion.

Concrete will shrink due to a combination of moisture loss from the surface and thermal contraction. Drying shrinkage will cause cracks spaced a few meters apart to appear in transversal direction. These are natural contraction (shrinkage) joints. Shrinkage cracks are tight when they form at first, but they open more with time—having larger width in winter, when maximum thermal contraction takes place.

Depending on the season the concrete is cast, net contraction or net expansion at the crack prevail alternatively (Figure 4). In winter:

(i)   newly cast concrete shrinks by losing moisture first and, after an initial thermal expansion caused by the internal heat of hydration of cement, it will cool (hence, it will shrink) rapidly to ambient temperature; and

(ii)   concrete is in *maximum contraction.*

After a few months, shrinkage decreases and movements are mainly dominated by expansion caused by the increasing temperature in passing from winter to summer (Figure 4). In summer:

(i)   newly cast concrete shrinks but because ambient temperature is high, thermal contraction is low;

(ii)   the amount of thermal expansion will generally overcome the amount of shrinkage contraction; and

(iii)   concrete is in maximum expansion.

Once formed, transversal joints will control contraction and expansion by opening and closing, so joints will be at maximum opening in winter and at minimum opening in summer. The equation to calculate joints opening ΔL for a distance L between two consecutive joints is given below (for symbols refer to Table 1):

$$\Delta L = C \cdot L(\alpha \Delta T + \varepsilon) \textbf{ eq-1}$$

The output of this equation is very sensitive to the coefficient of thermal expansion of concrete (CTE) α and to the drying shrinkage value of concrete ε. It may cause joint opening to be underestimated when non-realistic values of CTE and shrinkage are used. CTE expresses the unit elongation or contraction that concrete can undergo under a unit variation of temperature. Shrinkage expresses the amount of contraction that concrete can undergo when moisture is lost (mainly) from its surface due to evaporation.

CTE cannot be controlled, being a fundamental property of the aggregates used in concrete, while shrinkage will be reduced dramatically if proper curing is used in the first days. Chapter 2 gives guidance on the selection of values of CTE for different aggregate types.

Despite limestone having in general lower CTE than granite, it is not recommended to assume for the design of joints the values of: $6.0 \frac{\mu\varepsilon}{°C}$ and $8.0 \frac{\mu\varepsilon}{°C}$. Unless this parameter has been tested for local concrete, the general rule for CTE is to assume design values of $10.0 \frac{\mu\varepsilon}{°C}$ (or 10E-6/°C) regardless of the mineralogy of the aggregates used in the concrete.

Based on practical experience, the recommended conservative value for shrinkage to be used for design is 400 $\mu\varepsilon$ (or 0.04%). The calculated joint opening for L = 6.0 meters (m) can be as high as 2.5 millimeters (mm) in continental climate assuming the above values of CTE and shrinkage.

This means that in maximum contraction, joints can receive sand particles flushed by water over the pavement. This is called incompressible material and when the joint closes back in the summer, it restrains free movement causing higher localized compressive stresses to arise. These may cause spalling and blowups.

Transversal contraction joint filled with sand, flushed by rain.
The loss of compressible material used to seal the joint leaves the
joint susceptible to deterioration.

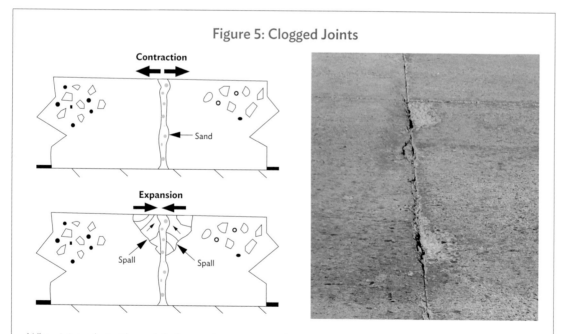

Figure 5: Clogged Joints

When joints clog with sand during maximum contraction, pavement expansion will be restrained in the summer and compressive forces cyclically applied to the face of the joint may cause spalling to form.

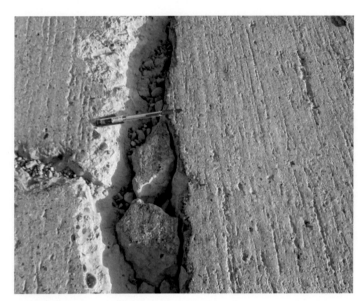

Compressive forces. Blown up at a transversal contraction joint caused by compressive forces.

Once cracked, the pavement will lose bearing capacity along the natural joints during maximum contraction. This is because the more crack walls separate from each other, the less friction is mobilized.

Usually for crack widths in excess of 1.5 mm, aggregate-to-aggregate interlock is lost and the load transfer efficiency (LTE) across the natural joint is reduced. Frictionless joints may cause adjacent slabs to vertically displace and create a type of distress called faulting.

Concrete cracks. The wall of a crack in concrete exposes aggregates that can contribute to friction only while the crack is tight (less than about 1.5 mm width).

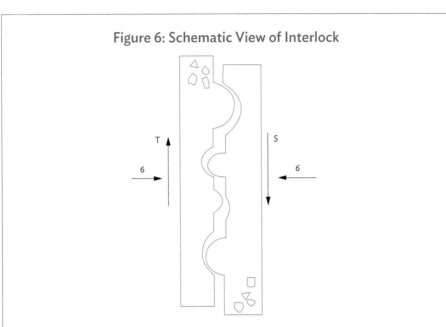

Figure 6: Schematic View of Interlock

As a result of friction between aggregates exposed on the opposite sides of the crack's wall, shear strength is mobilized.

Lack of load transfer. Faulting of a longitudinal joint caused by lack of load transfer (tie bars).

Hence, to avoid loss of load transfer capacity along natural joints, artificially controlled cracks are formed in JPCP by producing early saw cuts (i.e., a point of weakness) in the concrete and forcing transverse contraction cracks to appear in an ordered and controlled manner. In this way, the natural contraction joints are forced to form in predefined locations. The distance between two consecutive contraction joints formed by saw cut is called a slab or panel of length L.

Also, to avoid loss of bearing capacity across the joint, steel dowels are inserted during paving to ensure load transfer. These dowels must allow contraction and expansion of the crack from summer to winter and from winter to summer. Hence, they usually have one end greased to minimize friction with the concrete. For thicknesses of concrete of less than 28–30 centimeters (cm), the use of dowels must be carefully evaluated as they may promote cracking of thin concrete slabs.

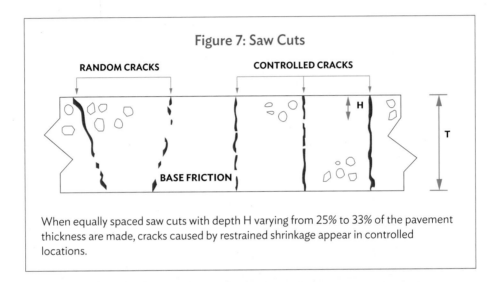

Figure 7: Saw Cuts

When equally spaced saw cuts with depth H varying from 25% to 33% of the pavement thickness are made, cracks caused by restrained shrinkage appear in controlled locations.

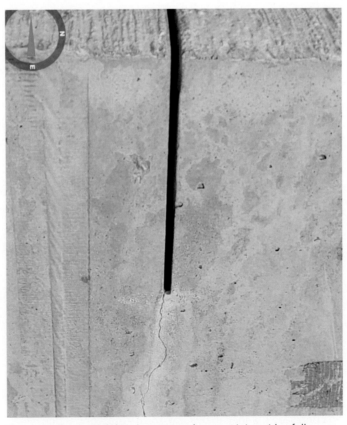

Transversal saw cut joint. A transversal saw cut joint with a fully formed, still tight crack.

For load transfer. Dowel basket assembly for load transfer efficiency across transversal contraction joints.

Figure 8: Dowelled Joint vs Undowelled Joint

When a joint is dowelled, the load applied on one side of the joint is resisted by the dowel. When a joint is not dowelled, the load applied on one side of the joint may cause vertical displacement along the joint's wall (faulting).

To ensure their functionality, dowels must be aligned to the horizontal plane to avoid restraint. If not properly aligned, dowels may cause structural cracks and spalling to form near the joint. Usually more than ±6.0 mm deviation from the horizontal plane is considered unacceptable for dowels' alignment.

Misaligned dowels. Misaligned dowels across the transverse contraction joint cause concrete to spall near the joint.

Spalls. One set of misaligned dowels across the transverse contraction joint causes concrete to spall near the joint.

Once the volumetric changes in the longest direction are controlled by early transversal saw cuts, which lead to a predefined spacing of transversal contraction joints, another type of deformation in the direction perpendicular to the paving direction should be controlled—warping or curling under temperature and moisture gradients within the concrete.

If a slab warps or curls, it loses support, hence, traffic repetitions can cause cracks to appear, where maximum tensile stresses occur.

These cracks will propagate and break the slab into pieces. To avoid this, the width of the carriageway is divided into longitudinal construction joints and across these joints, tie bars are installed. Tie bars are usually longer and of smaller diameter than dowels, but unlike dowels they must prevent bending of the slab, hence they are deformed for increased adhesion to concrete.

When temperature on the surface is lower than at the bottom (night) two adjacent slabs bend upward and they detach from ground of a distance L_{night}. When temperature is higher at the surface than the bottom (day) slabs bend downward, and they detach from the bottom of a distance L_{day}. Detached length can be calculated as a function of CTE (α), elastic modulus, thickness, temperature, and density of concrete. For the explanation of symbols refer to Table 2 (g = acceleration of gravity).

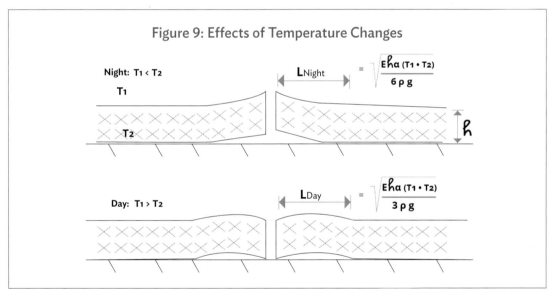

Figure 9: Effects of Temperature Changes

Night: $T_1 < T_2$
T_1

T_2

$$L_{Night} = \sqrt{\frac{Eh\alpha(T_1 \cdot T_2)}{6\rho g}}$$

h

Day: $T_1 > T_2$

$$L_{Day} = \sqrt{\frac{Eh\alpha(T_1 \cdot T_2)}{3\rho g}}$$

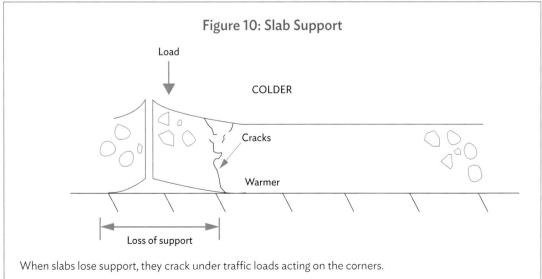

Figure 10: Slab Support

Load

COLDER

Cracks

Warmer

Loss of support

When slabs lose support, they crack under traffic loads acting on the corners.

Slab curling and warping. As a result of poor load transfer across the longitudinal construction joint, slabs curl and warp mainly under thermal cycles, losing support and cracking.

Figure 11: Joints Layout

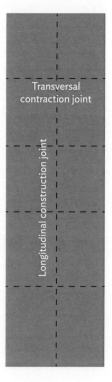

Transversal contraction joint

Longitudinal construction joint

To maximize load transfer efficiency and reduce the risk of loss of support through warping, transversal joints are cut and longitudinal construction joints are formed.

Figure 12: Allowing Load Transfer

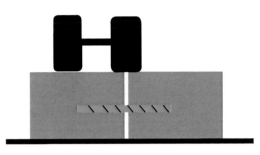

Dowels allow load transfer across the cracked transversal joint, while tie bars prevent bending by holding together two adjacent strips of pavement separated by a construction joint

Figure 13: Slab Length

Joint Spacing versus Foundation Stiffness

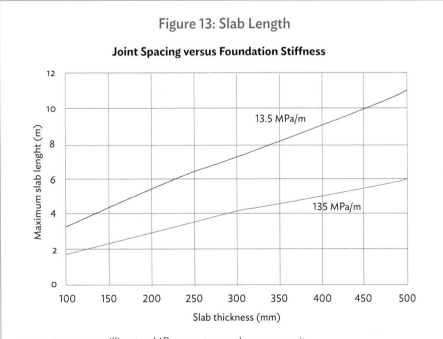

m = meter, mm = millimeter, MPa = megapascal pressure unit.

Chart for calculating slab length as a function of slab thickness and stiffness of the foundation.

The final pattern created by cutting transversal contraction joints and by forming longitudinal construction joints is called joints spacing (Figure 11). Joints spacing depends on the strength of the support and the thickness of the slab. The rule of thumb is that maximum spacing in meters (m) should equal 20 times thickness in millimeters (mm).

A more detailed correlation is presented in Figure 13 where, depending on support stiffness (recommended to be 130 megapascal pressure unit (MPa)/m for cement stabilized granular materials) the joints spacing can be determined for varying slab thickness. From Figure 13 it can be seen that the stiffer the support, the shorter the joints spacing should be. This is because internal stresses building up in the concrete exposed to the environment depend also on the strength of the support. Stronger support increases surface tensile stresses and vice versa.

C. Basic Design Principles

The design of JPCP is based on the concept of a rigid plate resting over springs—the rigid plate being the concrete slab and the springs being the foundation (support) over which concrete is placed (Figure 14).

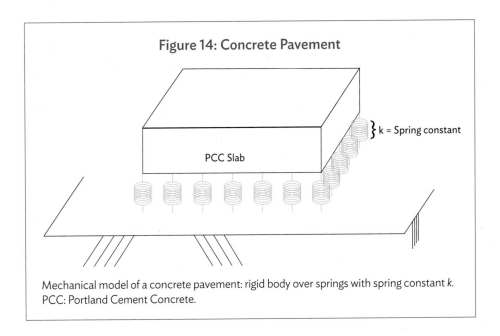

Figure 14: Concrete Pavement

PCC Slab

} k = Spring constant

Mechanical model of a concrete pavement: rigid body over springs with spring constant *k*.
PCC: Portland Cement Concrete.

For any external load applied by a vehicle, there will be internal stresses building up. Given the geometry of pavements, the most critical stresses to cause cracking are tensile stresses. Tensile stresses form, for instance, in the bottom half of a concrete slab loaded on the surface by a vehicle (Figure 15). Also, tensile stresses arise when pavements curl and warp under thermal and moisture gradients.

Concrete pavements are designed based on thickness and a characteristic flexural tensile strength. Flexural strength of concrete is determined usually with the American Society for Testing and Materials (ASTM) C78 method. This method simulates the mechanism of flexion that a concrete pavement is subjected to. The upper half of the beam subjected to bending is in compression and the bottom half is in tension. When tensile stresses at the bottom equal the flexural tensile strength (or modulus of rupture), the specimen will break (Figure 16). The crack will form at the base and it will propagate upward.

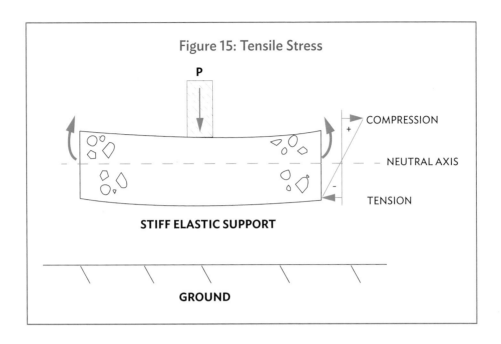

Figure 15: Tensile Stress

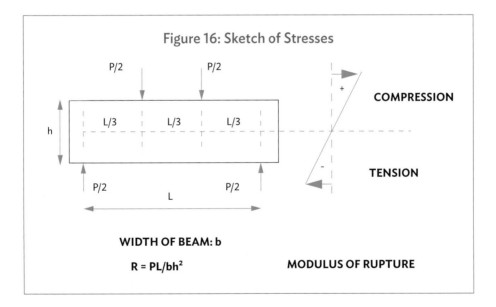

Figure 16: Sketch of Stresses

The thickness of concrete pavement is important because concrete pavements spread loads with depth, and the greater the depth, the larger the area the load is spread over (Figure 17).

Because load divided by area is equal to the applied stress, pavements have lower stresses at the bottom when they have greater thicknesses. However, it is not practical either from a construction or from a financial standpoint to increase the thickness of the pavement until tensile stresses at the bottom of the pavement become negligible. The design of concrete pavements is always therefore a tradeoff between thickness and flexural strength.

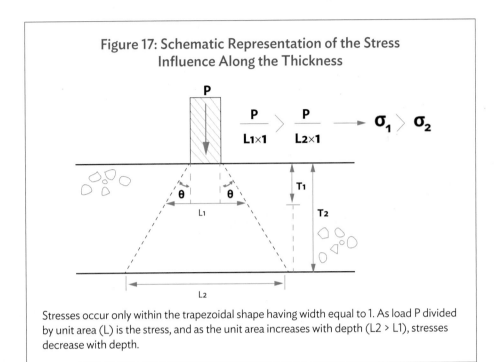

Figure 17: Schematic Representation of the Stress Influence Along the Thickness

Stresses occur only within the trapezoidal shape having width equal to 1. As load P divided by unit area (L) is the stress, and as the unit area increases with depth (L2 > L1), stresses decrease with depth.

The aim of pavement design is to:

(i)   calculate the maximum tensile stresses forming anywhere in the pavement due to traffic,
(ii)   calculate thermal stresses,
(iii) define a minimum flexural strength of the concrete to resist external stresses, and
(iv)   define a minimum thickness of concrete to minimize tensile stresses.

To define the minimum flexural strength, the maximum stresses from traffic and thermal loads must be calculated as will be shown later. Stresses on pavements are repeated. For instance, traffic causes loading and unloading of the pavement many times in a day and thermal gradients cause tensile stresses to cyclically form and disappear under varying ambient temperature.

Traffic repetitions might be in the order of the tens of million over the service life of the pavement, while generally heat/cold, dry/wet repetitions are much less frequent (few hundreds only over the service life).

The general rule in concrete pavement design is that as long as the ratio between applied stress by traffic loads and flexural tensile strength (also called stress ration [SR]) is less than 0.45, load repetitions on a concrete pavement of given thickness can be infinite without cracking.

When, however, applied stresses are 0.8 or more than flexural tensile strength, only a few hundred repetitions are allowed before cracking. This is the case for thermal stresses, which are usually larger in magnitude than traffic stresses but repeated much less frequently.

Figure 18 shows the permitted number of repetitions of loads as a function of the SR. At high SRs, only few hundreds of repetitions are possible before cracking, while for an SR of less than 0.45, repetitions can be in the order of tens of millions. In Figure 18, there are different curves, whereas the 95% reliability curve is the most conservative in terms of allowable SR at any given number of repetitions. Using a 95% reliability curve means that it is assumed that only 2.5 times out of 100, SRs will be lower than predicted by the curve for any given number of repetitions.

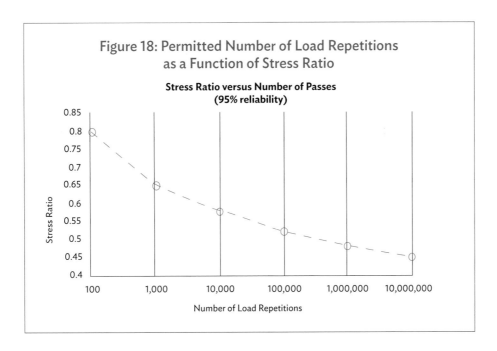

Figure 18: Permitted Number of Load Repetitions as a Function of Stress Ratio

D. The Nature of Stresses in Concrete Pavements

A slab of concrete in service is subjected to three main sources of stress:

(i)   stresses caused by the environment,
(ii)   stresses caused by friction with the underlying materials, and
(iii)   stresses caused by traffic.

Depending on where they act, these stresses may have varying intensity. The stresses that are of concern are solely tensile stresses as the mode of failure of concrete pavements is generally by tension-flexure. We divide critical positions where loads can be applied as corner, edge, interior (Figure 19).

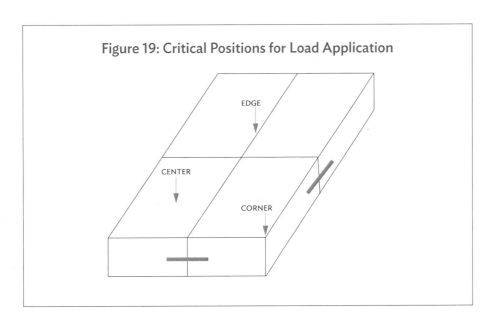

Figure 19: Critical Positions for Load Application

Environment

Any time the surface of a concrete pavement is heated more than the bottom, it will curl (or warp) and bend downward and vice versa (Figure 18). Bending induces internal tensile stresses. Curling upward may cause loss of support near corners with pumping and/or cracking.

Because curling and warping induced by the environment are seasonal, only few hundreds of repetitions of curling or warping events are expected during the service life of the pavement and usually these repetitions are negligible compared to traffic repetitions. Hence, if predicted internal stresses caused by curling and warping are lower than flexural strength by a factor of at least 0.8, they are not expected to be critical for cracking.

Corner support. Loss of corner support may cause water and silt or clay to be pumped upward by the repetitive deflection of the corner under traffic.

Loss of corner support. Loss of corner support may cause corner cracks to appear.

There are two equations for calculating the stresses induced by thermal gradients (Bradbury, 1938 for the meaning of symbols refer to Table 2):

$$\text{warping stress (edge loading)} = \frac{CE\alpha\Delta T}{2} \text{ - } \mathbf{eq\text{-}2}$$

$$\text{warping stress (interior loading)} = \frac{E\alpha\Delta T}{2(1\text{-}v^2)} (C_x + \upsilon C_y) \text{ - } \mathbf{eq\text{-}3}$$

where: C_x and C_y are shape factors.

Friction

A foundation's movement will be restrained by the friction between the concrete and the support (Figure 20). Concrete shrinks when it loses moisture or when it cools down (at night or in winter) or thermally expands (in summer).

This restrained contraction or expansion will cause internal tensile stresses to build up. However, the magnitude of these stresses is usually negligible, especially when the bond between concrete and support is minimized by use of bond breakers such as plastic sheets.

The equation for tensile stress induced by friction is

$$\sigma = \frac{\gamma_c L f_a}{2} \text{ - } \mathbf{eq\text{-}4}$$

Refer to tables 1 and 2 for the symbols used.

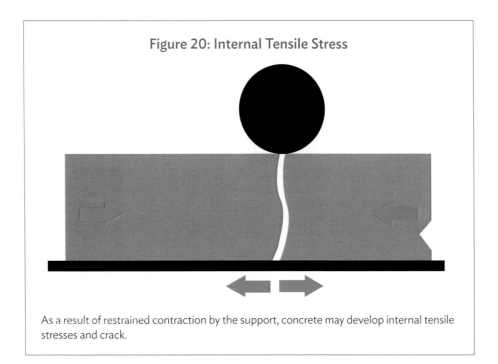

Figure 20: Internal Tensile Stress

As a result of restrained contraction by the support, concrete may develop internal tensile stresses and crack.

Traffic

Since the 1920s, the equations developed by Westergaard (1926) have represented the most widely used approach to the analysis of loaded concrete pavements. The original equations were derived assuming a concrete pavement to act as a slab in pure bending, and several subsequent modifications have been made over the years to increase the accuracy with which a real pavement can be modeled.

The equations are in terms of the maximum tensile stress in the concrete due to slab bending, and they are for three load locations:

(i)   one for corner loading,
(ii)   one from interior loading, and
(iii) one for edge loading.

$$\text{stress from corner loading: } \frac{3P}{h^2}\left[1-\left(\frac{C}{1}\right)^{0.72}\right] \textbf{eq-5}$$

$$\text{stress from interior loading: } \frac{3(1+\upsilon)P}{2\pi h^2}\left(\ln\frac{1}{b} + 0.6159\right) \textbf{eq-6}$$

$$\text{stress from edge loading: } \frac{3(1+\upsilon)P}{\pi(3+\upsilon)h^2}\left[\ln\left(\frac{Eh^3}{100ka^4}\right) + 1.84 - \frac{4\upsilon}{3} + \frac{1-v}{2} + \frac{1.18(1+2\upsilon)a}{1}\right] \textbf{eq-7}$$

Table 1: Symbols Used in Calculations for Stresses in Pavements

E	modulus of elasticity
υ	Poisson coefficient
α	coefficient of thermal expansion/contraction
1	radius of relative stiffness (refer to table 2)
k	value of soil reaction
h	concrete thickness
a	radius of contact area
P	applied traffic load
ΔT	thermal differential or thermal gradient depending on the equation
c	restraint factor (0.65 for stabilized base, or 0.80 for unbound base)
f_a	friction coefficient slab/support
C_x, C_y	shape factors (determined graphically)

Usually, the worst condition for traffic load is edge loading. Hence, edge loading is considered as the source of the critical tensile stress to be compared to flexural strength, to predict the number of possible repetitions before failure. The design axle load for heavily trafficked concrete roads can be as high as 130 kilonewtons (kN). This means that each axle of the truck is loaded with 130 kN.

For heavily loaded vehicles load is spread over tandems (twin tires per tandem as shown in photo), hence, the equivalent contact area of the tandem must be calculated.

Dual tandem trailers. These vehicles are designed for heavy load transfers.

An axle of heavy loaded truck has two tandem tires. One tandem can be sketched (Figure 21). Tires are spaced at a distance S_d and have length L with width of 0.6L. If q is the tire pressure, P is the load acting over the tandem (which is the design axle load divided by two) the radius a of the equivalent contact circular area of the tandem acting over the pavement is given by:

$$a = \sqrt{\frac{0.8521P_d}{q\pi} + \frac{S_d}{\pi}\left(\frac{P_d}{0.5227q}\right)^{1/2}} \text{ eq-8}$$

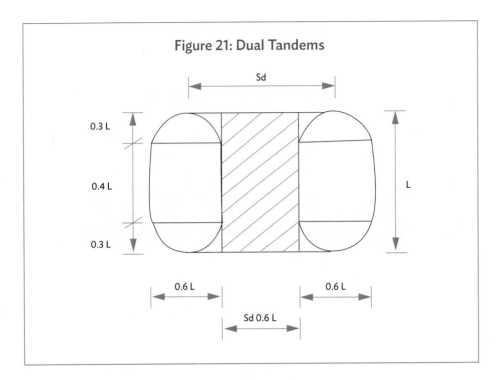

E. Input Parameters for Thickness Design

The indicative design input parameters that are important for calculating stresses on a pavement exposed to 130 kN axle load spread by dual tandem tires are summarized in Table 2.

F. Important Results from Thickness Design

Tables 3 and 4 report the output of the calculation of thermal stresses and stresses induced by a 130 kN load distributed over dual tandem tires as a function of the joints' spacing and thickness with the input values of Table 2.

From Tables 3 and 4, we can observe the following. If 6.0 m x 6.0 m is the joints spacing and the thickness of the slab is 250 mm, the maximum tensile stress from thermal loads is 3.09 MPa (interior curling stress), while the maximum tensile stress from traffic loads is 2.0 MPa (edge loading stress).

To account for fatigue and allow large load repetitions by traffic we need to consider a SR equal or less than 0.45.

$$SR = \frac{acting\ tensile\ stress}{flexural\ tensile\ stress} \leq 0.45$$

If the acting tensile stress induced by traffic loads is 2.0 MPa at the edge, a very large number of load repetitions (tens of millions) will be ensured when the resisting flexural tensile strength is ≥ 4.44 MPa. For lower repetitions of loads induced by thermal stresses the stress ratio can be as high as 0.80. If the acting tensile stress induced by thermal loads is 3.09 MPa (interior), a limited number of load repetitions will be ensured when the resisting flexural tensile strength is ≥ 3.9 MPa.

Table 2: Input Parameters for Calculating Stresses on Pavements

Parameter	Symbol	Units	Design Value	Notes	Application
Modulus of elasticity	E	GPa	27.6	When nothing else is known, 27.6 GPa should be a design value	To calculate stresses and deflections on corner, edge and interior
Poisson coefficient	υ	--	0.15		To calculate stresses and deflections on corner, edge and interior
Modulus of subgrade reaction	k	MPa/m	135	Assume high stiffness from a cement-treated foundation	To calculate stresses on corner, edge and interior
Coefficient of thermal expansion	α	$\mu\varepsilon$ °C	10.0		To calculate joints opening
Slab's thickness	h	m or mm	variable	Depends on expected loads	
Slab's length in transversal direction -	L_y	m or mm	variable	--	
Slab's Length in in longitudinal direction -	L_x	m or mm	variable	--	
Correction factors for the finite slab in the transversal direction	C_y	--	variable (depends on L_x)	Bradbury correction factor (1938) for = $L_x - L_y$	To apply shape correction factors to slabs geometry
Correction factors for the finite slab in the longitudinal direction	C_x	--	variable (depends on L_y)		
Radius of relative stiffness of the slab	l	m or mm	variable	$l = \left[\dfrac{Eh^3}{12(1-v^2)k} \right]^{0.25}$	
Contact pressure	q	kPa	variable		
Full weight on axle load (dual tandem)	P	kN	130.0	Assumed 130 kN axle load distributed by a trailer with dual tandem tires	To calculate stresses on the corner, edge, and interior
Concentrated load on the single tandem	P_0	kN	65.0		
Equivalent contact radius of the tandem	a	mm	198		To calculate stresses on the corner, edge, and interior
Unit weight of concrete	γ_c, ρ	kN/m³	2.4		To calculate friction with the base
Drying shrinkage of concrete	ε_d	$\mu\varepsilon$	400	1-year value based on experience for medium strength unreinforced concrete	To calculate joints opening
Maximum differential between time of concrete placement and minimum ambient temperature	ΔT	°C	40.0	Variable (depending on climate conditions, assume ≥ 40°C for continental climate)	To calculate joints opening
Thermal gradient in concrete from top to bottom	ΔT_c	°C / mm	0.007	The simplest assumption is to consider the gradient linear	To calculate warping and curling stresses

GPa = Giga pascal, kN = kilonewton, kPa = Kilo pascal, m = meter, mm = millimeter, MPa = megapascal pressure unit.

Note: For symbols used, refer to Table 1.

Table 3: 6x6-Meter Thermal and Traffic Stresses

6x6 Meter	Slab Thickness (millimeters)					
	200	225	250	275	300	325
Edge Curling Sress	2.1	2.37	2.63	2.89	3.16	3.42
Interior Curling Stress	2.48	2.78	3.09	3.4	3.71	4.02
Corner Loading Stress	1.6	1.43	1.26	1.12	1.00	0.89
Interior Loading Stress	1.61	1.34	1.13	0.96	0.83	0.72
Edge Loading Stress	2.79	2.34	2.0	1.73	1.51	1.34

Note: Values in red are thermal and blue are traffic stresses in megapascal pressure unit (MPa).

Table 4: 5x5-Meter Thermal and Traffic Stresses

5x5 Meter	Slab Thickness (millimeters)					
	200	225	250	275	300	325
Edge Curling Sress	1.89	2.13	2.37	2.6	2.84	3.08
Interior Curling Stress	2.23	2.51	2.78	3.06	3.34	3.62
Corner Loading Stress	1.6	1.43	1.26	1.12	1.00	0.89
Interior Loading Stress	1.61	1.34	1.13	0.96	0.83	0.72
Edge Loading Stress	2.79	2.34	2.0	1.73	1.51	1.34

Note: Values in red are thermal and blue are traffic stresses in megapascal pressure unit (MPa).

Hence, choosing a minimum value of flexural tensile strength of 4.44 MPa is suitable for a 6.0x6.0 m joints layout and a pavement thickness of 250 mm.

For the same joints spacing, we can also see that a pavement with 300 mm thickness receives lower edge tensile stresses induced by traffic (1.51 MPa) but larger tensile stresses induced by thermal loads (3.71 MPa, interior) than a 250 mm thick pavement. The minimum flexural tensile strength of fatigue induced by thermal loads increases therefore to minimum 4.6 MPa.

The minimum value of flexural tensile strength is determined in the laboratory by means of testing of a large population of data (usually from 15 beams and above) from a certain concrete mix design. Usually, in structural engineering, it is assumed that the minimum value or (characteristic value) for laboratory-tested strength of concrete is the value below which only 5% of results are (also called 90% confidence level).

When the average value (A) and standard deviation (S) of a large population of data of laboratory-tested concrete strength is known, the characteristic (K) value with 90% confidence level is given by:

$$K = A - 1.64 \cdot S$$

However, samples cast and cured in laboratory conditions will develop a potential strength that cannot usually be achieved on site due to lesser compaction and curing efficiency. Hence, the characteristic laboratory value shall be increased to account for some loss of strength when moving from characteristic strength in the lab to characteristic strength in the structure. We define the ratio $K_{lab} = \frac{K}{0.85}$ as the target characteristic strength in the laboratory.

Thus, for the example of a 250 mm thick slab with 6.0x.6.0 m joints spacing, the target characteristic flexural strength in the laboratory must be minimum 5.22 MPa if the minimum flexural strength to resist tensile stresses in the pavement is 4.44 MPa. Experience shows that to consistently achieve such characteristic strength an average strength of (K_{lab} + 0.7 MPa) is required to account for variations in test results.

Finally, the target average flexural strength of concrete in the laboratory shall be 5.92 MPa to obtain a satisfactory minimum value of flexural strength of 4.44 MPa in the 250 mm thick pavement with 6.0 m joints spacing.

Results from calculations of stresses on a 5.0x5.0 m joints spacing for varying concrete thicknesses are finally provided in Table 4 for comparison with Table 3.

2

Influence of Aggregates on Concrete Pavement Performance

A. Introduction and Overview

Concrete for pavements is a mixture of cement, water, aggregates, and specific chemical admixtures. Aggregates (making up for about 70%–80% of the volume of the concrete for pavements) of marginal quality contribute largely to defective concrete in the fresh state causing, for instance, segregation (that leads to plastic cracking, as discussed in Chapter 6), and/or in service, because of marginal strength and low resistance to freeze-thaw for example (structural cracking, scaling, or polishing).

There are, on the other hand, usually fewer cases of defective concrete resulting from the choice of the type of cement. Guidance on the suitability or unsuitability of different cement for concrete pavements is beyond the scope of this guide and it may be found in the selected literature provided in the appendix.

This section provides guidance in minimizing defects in concrete pavements that may be caused by aggregates and by how they are proportioned. The influence of chemical admixtures and water content will be discussed in detail in Chapter 3.

B. Aggregates-Related Defects in Concrete Pavements

The most common defects in built concrete pavements exposed to continental climate (having high seasonal and day-to-night temperature excursions) are shown in the photos. For example, improper proportioning of aggregates in concrete can cause segregation that can lead, for instance, to early surface polishing.

The most common aggregates-induced defects include:

(i)   map-cracking or D-cracking,
(ii)   surface scaling,
(iii)   polishing,
(iv)   pop-ups, or
(v)   segregation.

(i) D-cracking

(ii) moderate surface scaling

(iii) severe surface scaling

(iv) very severe surface scaling

(v) polished surface

(vi) pop-ups

Common aggregates-induced defects. Examples of common aggregates-induced defects include (i) D-cracking, (ii) moderate surface scaling, (iii) severe surface scaling, (iv) very severe surface scaling, (v) polished surface, and (vi) pop-ups.

Concrete for pavements with excess volume of sand (segregated). Segregated concrete core from a 20 mm maximum aggregate size concrete for pavements with excess volume of sand. The top part of the core has more paste and less coarse grains.

Concrete for pavements with balanced volume of sand (homogeneous). Homogeneous concrete core from the same 20 mm maximum aggregate size concrete for pavements with balanced volume of sand. The top part of the core has less paste and more coarse grains.

Disorders from alkali-silica or alkali-carbonate reactions may also cause pavements to crack and lose bearing capacity in the long term, but they are beyond the scope of this document. However, a list of potentially reactive rocks and aggregates is given and briefly discussed here. Except for segregation, the above defects are all strictly linked to the quality of aggregates.

C. Influence of Aggregates on Some Key Properties of Concrete

About 70%–80% of the volume of concrete for pavements is occupied by aggregates (coarse and fine aggregates), which means that the quality of aggregates will have a major influence on the performance of concrete in the fresh and hardened state. The major aggregate-related parameters for a concrete mix for pavements to perform satisfactorily in service are:

(i)   aggregates petrography;
(ii)   deleterious materials in aggregates;
(iii)   aggregates absorption;
(iv)   aggregates strength;
(v)   aggregates shape; and
(vi)   aggregates grading, workability factor and coarseness factor, and maximum aggregate size.

Petrography

Petrography defines the mineralogical composition of rocks as observed on field samples or under the microscope in the laboratory. It is beyond the scope of this document to provide extensive information on the geological setting of aggregate-forming rocks.

For the time being, it suffices to acknowledge that main rock types on Earth are either formed by solidified magma or lava (igneous rocks), or by biochemical processes promoted by marine organisms (biogenic sedimentary rocks), or by transport processes associated with moving fluids (such as water and air) that deposit particles in basins where they set and harden with natural cement dissolved in waters (terrigenous sedimentary rocks).

Aggregates for concrete are, except for those produced from manufactured materials (expanded clay, slag, etc.), always obtained by one of the above rock types. The way rocks are formed and the type of minerals they contain dictate how they behave when processed into aggregates for concrete.

Four main rock families are differentiated based on the main mineral components and genesis:

(i) **Acid igneous rocks:** made out of a combination of quartz, feldspar, and plagioclase (sodium-potassium silicates) with minor components (also known as accessory minerals). Examples of acid igneous rocks are: granite, granodiorite, quartzite, tuff, rhyolite.

(ii) **Basic igneous rocks:** do not contain significant quartz, but contain abundant feldspar, plagioclase, and other magnesium and iron bearing minerals (olivine, pyroxene, etc.). Examples of basic igneous rocks are: basalt, gabbro, diorite, dolerite (diabase), andesite, dacite (Figure 38).

(iii) **Sedimentary rocks:** made either from fossil microorganisms (common rocks: limestone and dolomite made entirely by calcite and dolomite minerals and subordinate siliceous cement) or formed by accumulations of grains eroded from other rocks (sandstone, siltstone). In the first case, the main composition of the rock is either calcium carbonate or dolomite both as grains and as cement holding the grains together, in the second case the mineral grains can be eroded from any source (igneous, sedimentary...) and they are bonded together by a natural calcite and/or siliceous cement. Unlike igneous rocks that are generally massive, sedimentary rocks are found in strata or beds with thickness varying from few millimeters to tens of meters (massive).

(iv) **Metamorphic rocks:** formed when pre-existing sedimentary and igneous rocks are subjected to extremely high pressure and temperature caused by crustal deformations related to plate tectonics in what we know as mountain building processes. These "new" rocks usually contain the original minerals of the parent rock they originate from, plus additional mineral phases formed during the process (chlorite, talc and micas being examples of newly formed species under the metamorphic process and being known to be among the deleterious components for concrete). Examples of these rock types are: gneiss, micaschist, quartzite, and marble.

Because of the very high energies experienced during their genesis causing them to strain and flow, metamorphic rocks have a so-called foliated structure favored by plate-like minerals such as micas and chlorite. This feature makes these rocks sometimes more susceptible to mechanical weakness and environmental weathering. Also, when granite or other rocks containing abundant quartz are subjected to metamorphism, quartz may get strained and become reactive to the alkalis of cement to cause disruptive reactions known as alkali-silica reactions.

Massive outcrop of granite. This massive outcrop of granite is from the Russian Federation.

Massive basalt lava flows. Formed from basalt lava flows in Ethiopia.

Calcium carbonate. Modern-day reefs are made entirely of calcium carbonate; as shown here in West Samoa.

Dolomite. The Dolomites mountain range in North of Italy is made entirely of fossil coral reefs.

Sandstone. Stratified sedimentary rocks found in Colorado.

Foliated grain of micaschist. A sample of foliated grain of micaschist.

A simple, yet illustrative diagram to understand the so-called rock cycle is given in Figure 22.

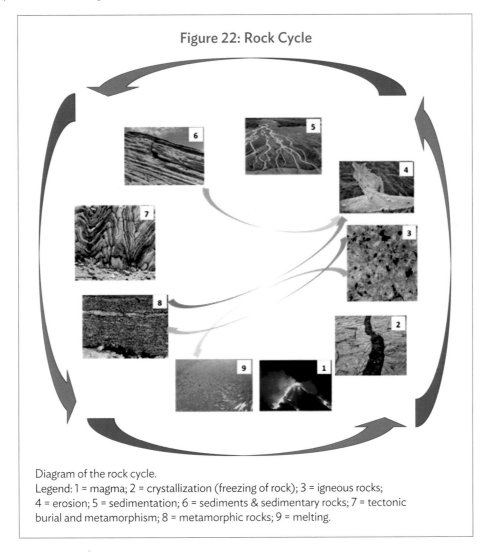

Figure 22: Rock Cycle

Diagram of the rock cycle.
Legend: 1 = magma; 2 = crystallization (freezing of rock); 3 = igneous rocks;
4 = erosion; 5 = sedimentation; 6 = sediments & sedimentary rocks; 7 = tectonic
burial and metamorphism; 8 = metamorphic rocks; 9 = melting.

Weathering of Rocks and Impact on Aggregates Quality

In general, when rocks are exposed to the environment (air, water) they weather. Weathering is a chemical–physical process whereby mechanical breaking (by heat–cold cycles, transport by water, transport by gravity through rock falls and rockslides, etc.) and chemical reactions concur in transforming most of the minerals in the rock into clay minerals.

Clay, in highly weathered rocks, may be found as a deleterious substance for the production of concrete. Thus, producing aggregates form weathered rocks is not advisable because of the amount of clay that they may contain. The presence of layers of clay in a quarry can cause formation of clay lumps and deleterious substances contaminating the resulting aggregates.

In visually evaluating the suitability of certain rock outcrops to be quarried for aggregates, one of the most important observations relates to the possibility of aggregates to be contaminated during blasting or digging operations by layers of weathered rocks and/or by clay seams and veins.

Front of a quarry in basalt rock formations on the island of West Samoa (Oceania). Dark gray blocks are non-weathered. Yellowish surface stains on the quarry face and on some blocks indicates slight weathering. Moving upward on the quarry face the amount of clay (darker color) increases till the upper part of the quarry is a layer of soil-like extremely weathered rock (saprolite).

Table 5 presents the different ideal degrees of weathering for a rock face. Aggregate quarrying should only take place in rocks classified as slightly weathered (II) to fresh (IA) to limit contamination by weak particles, as discussed later in this document.

Table 5: Weathering Scale for Rocks

Humus - Top soil	
VI - Residual Soil	All rock material converted to soil: mass structure and material fabric destroyed
V - Completely Weathered	All rock material decomposed and/or disintegrated to soil. Original mass structure still largely intact.
IV - Highly Weathered	More than 50% of rock material decomposed and/or disintegrated to soil. Fresh/discolored rock present as discontinous framework of corestones.
III - Moderately Weathered	Less than 50% of rock material decomposed and/or disintegrated to soil. Fresh/discolored rock present as discontinous framework of corestones.
II - Slightly Weathered	Discoloration indicates weathering of rock material and discontinuity surfaces. All rock material may be discolored by weathering and may be weaker than in the fresh condition.
IB - Faintly Weathered	Discoloration on major discontinuity surface
IA - Fresh	No visible sign of rock material weathering

The ultimate process of weathering is the substitution of most of the minerals in the parent rock by clay minerals. The result of this course is the formation of saprolite, which preserves a rock-like appearance while having the consistency of a soil that can be washed away by rain. Photos of basalt aggregates show the outcome of processing coarse aggregates from a clay contaminated (weathered) rock face and from a clean (fresh) rock face.

(i) saprolite

(ii) clay-coated basalt aggregates

(iii) clean basalt aggregates

(iv) natural river sand (3.0 mm maximum size)

(v) desert sand in Ethiopia's Rift Valley

(vi) quartz grains in river sand

(vii) river deposits of sand and gravel in coarser sizes from Azerbaijan

(viii) microscopic analysis of river sand with dominant quartz (qz) grains

(ix) lake sand in Ethiopia

Rocks and the weathering process.
Examples of rocks in various stages of the weathering process: (i) saprolite; (ii) clay-coated basalt aggregates; (iii) clean basalt aggregates; (iv) natural river sand (3.0 mm maximum size; (v) desert sand in Ethiopia's Rift Valley; (vi) quartz grains in river sand; (vii) river deposits of sand and gravel in coarser sizes from Azerbaijan; (viii) microscopic analysis of river sand with dominant quartz (qz) grains; and (ix) lake sand in Ethiopia.

Because quartz is resistant to chemical reactions with the environment, it survives weathering and it is transported downstream to form natural sand.

Thus, natural sand is a material made mostly of residual quartz grains with subordinate minerals that can all resist the chemical dissolution by water (feldspars, dolomite, etc.). Natural sand can be transported and deposited by wind (desert sand), by water in rivers or by water in lakes.

An important engineering outcome from the petrography and genesis of a rock is the coefficient of thermal expansion of aggregates (and concrete), which controls the joints opening of concrete pavements (Chapter 1).

Quartz-rich rocks (chert, some sandstones, quartzite, quartz-rich granite) have higher coefficient of thermal expansion (CTE) than rocks with a low content of this mineral and having higher content of iron- and magnesium-bearing minerals. Typical values, along with design values recommended for this parameter, are given in Table 5.

Table 6 describes the design values for granitic rocks that are as high as 10.5. Limestone varies from 9.0 to 10.5. However, the known range of values for each rock is much broader.

The reason for using design (i.e., conservative) values is related to the possibility of underestimating movements at the joints causing internal stresses to build up and inducing distresses in the pavement, such as faulting, cracking, and blowups (Chapter 1).

The last important consequence of the varying mineralogy and origin for the aggregate-making rocks is the impact they have on durability related to deleterious reactions between some forms of quartz and the alkalis in the cement (alkali-silica reactions, ASR) and some forms of dolomitic limestone and the alkalis in the cement (alkali-carbonate reactions, ACR) (Table 7).

Table 6: Coefficient of Thermal Expansion of Common Rocks, Aggregates, and Concrete

| Coarse Aggregate/ Rock Group | Coefficient of Thermal Expansion ($\mu\varepsilon/°C$) | | | |
| | | | Design Value | |
	Rock	Saturated Concrete	Sand from the same rock	Siliceous sand
Chert/flint	7.4-13.0	11.4-12.2	12	12
Quartzite	7.0-13.0	11.7-14.6	14	14
Sandstone	4.3-12.1	9.2-13.3	12.5	12.5
Marble	2.2-16.0	4.4-7.4	7	8
Siliceous limestone	3.6-9.7	8.1-11.0	10.5	11
Granite	1.8-11.9	8.1-10.3	10	10.5
Dolerite	4.5-8.5	9.2	9.5	10
Basalt	4.0-9.7	7.9-10.4	10	10.5
Limestone	1.8-11.7	4.3-10.3	9	9.5

Table 7: Common Alkali-Reactive Rocks and Minerals

Alkali-Silica Reactive Substances		Alkali-Carbonate Reactive Substances
Andesites	Opal	Calcitic dolomites
Argillites	Opaline shales	Dolomitic limestones
Certain siliceous limestones and dolomites	Phyllites	Fine-grained dolomites
Chalcedonic cherts	Quartzites	
Chalcedony	Cherts	
Cristobalite	Rhyolites	
Dacites	Schists	
Glassy or cryptocrystalline volcanics	Siliceous shales	
Granite gneiss	Strained quartz	
Metagraywackes	Tridymite	

Any time a petrographic analysis conducted according to one of the standards reported in Tables 12 and 13 shows potentially deleterious minerals for ASR or ACR, a more detailed investigation shall be implemented using specific tests which are beyond the scope of this document, but for which a selected literature is provided in the appendix to this handbook.

When rocks are prospected to produce aggregates, the petrography, mineral composition, and degree of weathering must be known, because from the knowledge of the composition, important information on the behavior of the concrete made with the selected aggregates can be obtained. This essential geological recognition does or does not trigger the need for further confirmatory testing.

Influence of Deleterious Substances in Aggregates on the Performance of Concrete

A list of the most common deleterious substances that can be found in aggregates either from internal contamination (crushing of weathered rocks or dredging of sand and coarse aggregates rich in organic material for instance) or from external contamination (wind-blown sulfates in desert areas for instance) is reported in Table 8.

When prospecting for a quarry and when the risk of contamination from deleterious substances is ascertained by observing the degree of weathering of the rock outcrops, washing of aggregates may be advisable to minimize the risk of undesirable quality problems with fresh and hardened concrete.

Clay coatings are by far the most common deleterious materials found especially in coarse aggregates quarried from weathered rocks, followed by organic material and weak/porous particles mostly accumulating in natural sand from low-energy rivers or lakes.

Sand from high-energy environments (rivers, sea shores) will be less contaminated because of the "cleansing effect" by flowing water. However, sand quarried from low-energy rivers, river-mouths, or lakes can also contain high content of organic material which can easily be detected visually being of typical brown color. A list of tests and limits for deleterious substances in aggregates is given in Tables 12 and 13.

Sample of river sand with high organic content. Before being used for concrete, river sand requires testing for organic content.

Table 8: Common Deleterious Substances in Aggregates for Concrete

	Possible Adverse Effects on Concrete[a]				
	i	ii	iii	iv	v
Clay coatings on aggregate particles	-	✓	-	-	-
Clay lumps and altered rock particles	-	-	✓	✓	✓✓
Absorptive and microporous particles	-	-	✓	✓	✓✓
Coal and lightweight particles	-	-	-	-	✓✓
Weak or soft particles and coatings	-	✓✓	✓	✓	✓✓
Organic matter	✓✓	-	✓	-	-
Mica	-	-	✓✓	-	✓
Chlorides[b]	-	-	-	✓	-
Sulfates	-	-	-	✓✓	✓
Pyrite (iron disulfide)	-	-	-	✓✓	✓✓
Soluble lead, zinc, or cadmium	✓✓	-	-	-	-
Alkali-reactive constituents	-	✓	-	✓✓	-
Releasable alkalis	-	-	-	✓✓	-

Notes:

(i)   Chemical interference with the setting of concrete
(ii) Physical prevention of good bond between the aggregate and the cement paste
(iii) Modifications of the properties of the fresh concrete to the detriment of the durability and strength of the hardened material
(iv) Interaction between the cement paste and the aggregate which continues after hardening, sometimes causing expansion and cracking of the concrete
(v)   Weakness and poor durability of the aggregate particles themselves

The main problem with chlorides in concrete is associated with the corrosion of embedded steel.

✓✓ main effect
✓ addition effect

Influence of Aggregates' Absorption on Concrete Properties

Because of natural porosity present in the rock and because of the mechanical processing of crushing, aggregates have some degree of absorption. Absorption is the amount of water that a given mass of bone-dry aggregates grains can absorb when immersed in water for 24 hours. Hence a mass of, say, 1,000 kilograms (kg) of aggregate with absorption of, say, 2.0% absorbs 20 liters of water. Chapter 3 explains the different moisture states in which aggregates can be found.

Fine and coarse aggregates will generally have absorption levels in the range of 0.2%to 4.0% and 0.2% to 2.0%, respectively. Although no universal rule can be applied, it is not recommended to use fine and coarse aggregates with absorption rates in excess of 4.0%, in general, and it is not advisable to use coarse aggregates with absorption of more than 2.0% specifically for concrete paving applications in regions with winter frost.

The importance of size and absorption cannot be overemphasized when attempting to evaluate the preliminary suitability of an aggregate to resist freeze-thaw. Only coarser fractions may lead to defective concrete by formation of D-cracks which are caused by freeze-thaw effect on aggregates.

Thus, a 20 mm aggregate size made from the same rock and having the same absorption, will be less prone to deterioration under freeze-thaw than, for example, a 40 mm size.

An aggregate produced from a hard rock with high compressive strength (in excess of 100 MPa) will generally be less porous than an aggregate produced from a weaker rock. Hence, high-strength rocks generally produce less porous aggregates.

The more water is absorbed by the aggregate either during production and stockpiling (from washing and/or exposure to rain) or in service, and the coarser the aggregate is, the more likely it will result in poor service performance when it comes to frost conditions.

Water absorbed by aggregates will freeze and expand during a cold cycle, causing internal pressure to develop and the aggregate to expand and crack. This expansion causes also the paste surrounding the coarsest aggregates to crack, especially toward less restrained areas of the pavements such as joints. This is called map-cracking or D-cracking. A list of tests and limits for absorption of aggregates is given in Tables 13 and 14.

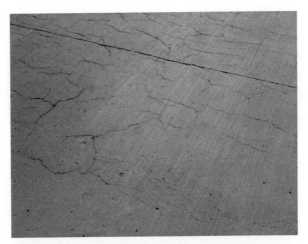

D-cracking. D-cracking caused by expansion of coarse aggregates under frost conditions in proximity of a transversal construction joint.

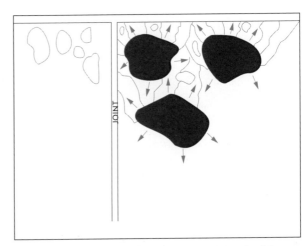

Expansion of coarse aggregates. Idealized sketch of the expansion of coarse aggregates under frost conditions with rupture of the paste toward the less restrained joint's wall and formation of cracks emerging on the surface as D-crack.

Strength of Aggregates

The strength of the rock the aggregate is quarried from will largely dictate whether the single aggregates grains will be strong, resistant to abrasion, durable, etc. Aggregates for concrete pavements must be strong and resistant to traffic abrasion and, in certain climates, they must be resistant to freeze-thaw as well.

The strength of rocks can be assessed in the field using a geological hammer a pocket knife, or using a point load apparatus.

Point load test (ASTM D5731) requires a portable and inexpensive equipment that can be used to test cylindrical specimens or blocks of regular and irregular shape. The point load index (PL_{index}) is converted to uniaxial compressive strength (UCS) using the following relationship: $UCS = K \cdot PL_{index}$

Where K is an integer number that varies from a minimum of 15 to a maximum of 25 depending on available data in the literature with a recommended conversion value between 20 and 25.

Uniaxial compressive strength can only be determined in the laboratory but it is generally not required once a proper geological assessment of the quarry is made and field tools (hammer and pocket knife) are used to estimate strength.

Table 9 presents the classification of strength of rocks based on field tests (blows, scratch, and point load) and laboratory tests (uniaxial compressive strength).

Geological hammer. This is one of the tools that may be used for assessing the strength of rocks.

Point load test on a core. The force required to break the core divided by the distance between the two loading ends is the point load index.

Point load test on a block. The force required to break the core divided by the distance between the two loading ends is the point load index.

Table 9: Classification of the Strength of Rocks

Grade	Classification	Field Identification	Uniaxial Compressive Strength	Point Load
R0	Extremely weak	Indented by thumbnail	< 1 MPa	N/A
R1	Very weak	Crumble under firm blows of geological hammer, can be peeled with a pocket knife	1-5 MPa	N/A
R2	Weak	Can be peeled with a pocket knife with difficulty; shallow indentations made with a firm blow with point of geological hammer	5-25 MPa	N/A
R3	Moderately strong	Cannot be scraped or peeled with a pocket knife; specimen can be fractured with a single firm blow of geological hammer	25-50 MPa	1-2 MPa
R4	Strong	Specimen requires more than one blow of geological hammer to fracture	50-100 MPa	2-4 MPa
R5	Very strong	Specimen requires many blows of geological hammer to fracture	100-250 MPa	4-10 MPa
R6	Extremely strong	Specimen can only be chipped with the geological hammer	>250 MPa	>10 MPa

MPa = megapascal pressure unit, N/A = not applicable.

Usually rocks in the class from R4 and above are suitable for producing aggregates for concrete from a strength standpoint. Grains of aggregates produced from a rock with a given strength can also be tested for their individual strength using toughness or abrasion tests.

There are many tests devised to determine the toughness of aggregates, and one of the most common, simple, and inexpensive is the Los Angeles Abrasion test (ASTM C131, EN 1097-2). In this laboratory test, a sample of coarse aggregate of a certain size range is subjected to a given number of revolutions in a rotating drum charged with steel balls (abrasive charge).

The percentage of material passing the 1.7 mm sieve that formed under a given number of revolutions and a given mass of abrasive charge is defined as the Los Angeles abrasion value, or simply the LA value. The lower the LA value, the stronger the aggregate generally is.

For example, an LA value of 40 (or LA_{40}) indicates that 40% of coarse aggregate grains tested, have reduced to less than 1.7 mm size after the predefined number of revolutions with the given charge.

For concrete pavements only aggregates with an LA equal or less to LA_{40} may be used, preferably, under LA_{30} for aggregates exposed to areas of freeze and thaw. A list of tests and limits for strength of aggregates in concrete is given in Table 13.

Los Angeles abrasion test apparatus. This is among the most common, simple, and inexpensive abrasion test equipment available in the market.

Abrasive charge. With the Los Angeles abrasion test, the sample is subjected to a given number of revolutions in a rotating drum charged with steel balls.

Grading of Aggregates

Fine and coarse aggregates for concrete are generally defined as aggregates with a maximum grain size of less than or more than 5.0 mm, respectively. Fine aggregates in this guide are also often referred to as "sand" as well.

Sieve sizes depend on the regulations in place in the country of production of the aggregates. Table 10 shows a comparison between sieve sizes adopted by ASTM C33, EN 12620, and Russian standards.

Noticeably, the last sieve, used to determine the size of dust-like particles defined in concrete technology as "fines," changes from standard to standard, and because some criteria for suitability of aggregates are based on a maximum percentage of fines, it is important to define what size is "fines."

In this guide, fines are intended, in accordance, with EN 12620 standard as the percentage passing 0.063 mm. However, given the proximity of size between 0.050 mm, 0.063 mm, and 0.075 mm, the term "fines" can be applied to all the above mentioned standards with the same meaning and practical technological implications.

Table 10: Comparison of Sieve Sizes

SIEVE SIZE (millimeters)		
ASTM	EN	GOST
37.5	40	40
–	31.5	–
25	–	–
–	20	20
19	–	–
–	16	–
12.5	–	–
–	10	10
9.5	–	–
–	8	–
–	–	5
4.75	–	–
–	4	–
–	–	2.5
2.36	–	–
–	2	–
1.18	–	–
–	1	–
0.6	–	–
–	–	0.63
–	0.5	–
0.3	–	–
–	0.25	–
–	–	0.16
0.15	–	––
–	0.125	
0.075 (fines)	–	–
–	0.063 (fines)	–
–	–	0.050 (fines)

Practical experience shows that when proportioning aggregates for concrete, the focus must first be on sand as far as dosage and grading properties are concerned.

Sand grading varies, depending on whether it is quarried from natural deposits (river beds, sea beds, or dunes) or crushed from blasted or broken rock fragments. Sand from natural deposits tend to be more uniform in size, while manufactured sand tends to be non-uniform and usually rich in quarry dust (i.e., fines as defined in this section). Uniformity is a measurement of how well represented each range of size is within the grading of the aggregate. A uniformly graded aggregate contains grain of all sizes within the grading, while a non-uniform aggregate will contain preferred sizes and lack partially or completely others.

Also, the fines content in natural sand is usually lower because of the generally high energy of the environment sand is deposited in, whereas in crushed sand, quarry dust formed during crushing operations tends to accumulate at the end of the process.

Usually, the quality of fines in natural sand is worse than crushed sand from non-weathered rocks. Natural sand, in fact, may contain clay and organic impurities (from decomposing plants and animal, or polluted waters), which may be deleterious for concrete production.

Crushed sand on the contrary contains quarry dust, which is a fine and generally non-deleterious product from the crushing of the rock. Sometimes, during the crushing of highly weathered rocks, clay may also contaminate crushed sand.

Experience shows that the target envelope of ASTM C33 for sand has provided good performance for many years for concrete pavements. The envelope is graphically presented in Figure 23 (blue lines) versus two examples of grading analysis of a uniform river sand and non-uniform crushed sand. Table 11 presents the entry data for the envelope.

ASTM C33 limits the quantity of particles passing 0.150 mm to 10%. For natural sand, ASTM accepts up to 3.0% "fines" (passing 0.075 mm), to be increased to 7.0% for crushed sand.

Quarry. Fresh blocks of a quarry face with clay-rich brownish horizons toward the top.

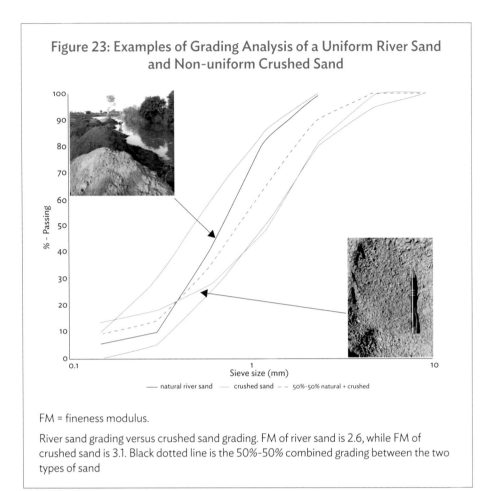

Figure 23: Examples of Grading Analysis of a Uniform River Sand and Non-uniform Crushed Sand

— natural river sand   — crushed sand – – 50%-50% natural + crushed

FM = fineness modulus.

River sand grading versus crushed sand grading. FM of river sand is 2.6, while FM of crushed sand is 3.1. Black dotted line is the 50%-50% combined grading between the two types of sand

Table 11: Entry Data of ASTM C33 Envelope for Sand

Sieve Size	Minimum	Maximum
9.5	100	100
4.75	95	100
2.36	80	100
1.18	50	85
0.600	25	60
0.300	5	30
0.150	0	10

One important parameter that allows to classify suitability of sand and which can be calculated from a grading curve made according to ASTM C33 standard is the fineness modulus (FM) defined as follows:

$$FM = \frac{\sum \%Retained\ (9.5+4.75+2.36+1.18+0.600+0.300+0.150)}{100} \text{ -eq-9}$$

A high FM means coarse sand and vice versa. Practice shows that sand with FM comprised between 2.4 and 3.4 and/or any combination thereof can produce acceptable concrete for paving.

Coarse aggregates for concrete mixes designed for pavements usually include 5–20 mm and, optionally, 20–40 mm ranges of sizes. Practical experience shows that the grading limits of Figure 24 provide aggregates with a good performance record. These limits are for uniformly graded aggregates with little oversize and undersize material at the control sieves of the grading class (5 mm, 20 mm, and 40 mm, respectively).

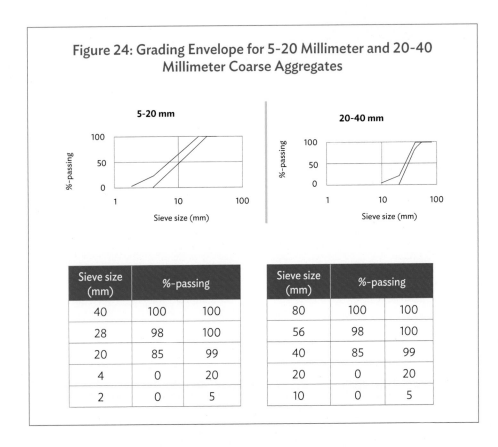

Figure 24: Grading Envelope for 5-20 Millimeter and 20-40 Millimeter Coarse Aggregates

5-20 mm

Sieve size (mm)	%-passing	
40	100	100
28	98	100
20	85	99
4	0	20
2	0	5

20-40 mm

Sieve size (mm)	%-passing	
80	100	100
56	98	100
40	85	99
20	0	20
10	0	5

The content of fines in coarse aggregates should be limited to 1.5% (Table 12) considering the environmental exposure of concrete pavements cold/continental climate and in accordance with ASTM C33.

The photos show a 10–20 mm gabbro aggregate (Dubai, UAE) coated with quarry dust, and a magnification (50x) under the microscope of this dust, which is made of gabbro and quartz grains. This is an example of non-deleterious clay-free fine material (quarry dust) generated from crushing and hauling of aggregates.

Experience with concrete pavements all around the world shows that, as proposed by Shilstone in 1990, when fine and coarse aggregates are combined to produce a combined grading for a mix design for concrete pavements, the governing factors on the performance of the concrete in terms of workability and resistance to segregation are the following:

(i)   % retained over 2.36 mm (or 2.5 mm for Russian standards),
(ii)   % passing 2.36 mm (or 2.5 mm for Russian standards), and
(iii) % retained over 9.5 mm (or 10.0 mm for Russian standards).

Gabbro aggregates. Coarse gabbro aggregates coated with quarry dust.

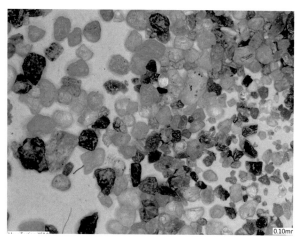

Magnified image under the microscope of the quarry dust from the gabbro. Grains are entirely made of gabbro, quartz, other minerals, and no clay.

The following two parameters can be introduced:

$$workability\ factor\ (WF) = \%\ passing\ 2.36\ mm\ (2.50\ mm)$$

$$coarseness\ factor\ (CF) = \frac{\%\ retained\ over\ 9.5\ mm\ (10.0\ mm)}{\%\ retained\ over\ 2.36\ mm\ (2.5\ mm)}$$

Practical experience shows that the best combination of fine and coarse aggregates for paving is that one comprised between two grading curves described by: WF = 45% and CF = 45% (fine) and WF = 30% and CF = 65% (coarse).

The objective of combining fine and coarse aggregates is to optimize packing of aggregates for the best result specially with slipform paving (reduce edge slump and minimize vertical segregation).

Aeronautical concrete pavement. Zero edge slump on a 0.5 m thick aeronautical concrete pavement with controlled CF and WF.

Slipform paving, especially, requires aggregates of smaller sizes to fill the voids left by aggregates of coarser size to create a stable skeleton.

When aggregates contain too many fines (in combination with an excessive amount of cement), fresh concrete may segregate under vibration causing a layer of sand and cement to form in the upper part of the pavement.

This layer can cause early cracking after few hours from placement (plastic shrinkage cracks), and/or it can rapidly abrade under traffic and reduce skid resistance with rain, causing hazardous conditions for travelers and expensive mechanical grooving to restore safety.

Concrete mix. Vertically segregated concrete mix containing excess fines and sand.

Poor aggregates proportioning. Polished concrete surface after 5 years in service only induced by a layer of segregated mortar caused by poor aggregates proportioning (excess sand).

Experience shows that the envelope provided in Figure 25 (blue lines) produces good concrete for pavements both with fixed-form and slipform techniques. For fixed-form the upper part (or the finer curve) of the envelope is recommended, while for slipform the lower part (or the coarser curve) of the envelope should be targeted. The envelope can be constructed from the values in Table 10.

In this respect, the grading envelope provided by NHK 87-13 permits very coarse blends of aggregates and very fine ones to be acceptable for paving (yellow regions in Figure 25).

These extreme limits are not recommended to be implemented for pavements. When blends are too coarse, finishing and brushing may be difficult, besides that the freeze-thaw resistance of the pavement might be compromised since it has been demonstrated by extensive studies in the last 50 years that coarser aggregates favor, keeping all other factors constant, D-cracking.

When blends are too fine, there is a risk of vertical segregation under vibration and, again, texturing of the concrete might be poor (surface roughness is low, traffic safety is low) and plastic shrinkage cracks may appear (Chapter 6). Concrete exposed to freeze-thaw should not contain (or it should contain in limited amount not exceeding 15% by mass of aggregates) 40 mm aggregates as the risk of D-cracking increases with the size, unless aggregates have been proven to be non-frost susceptible by one of the tests reported in Table 12.

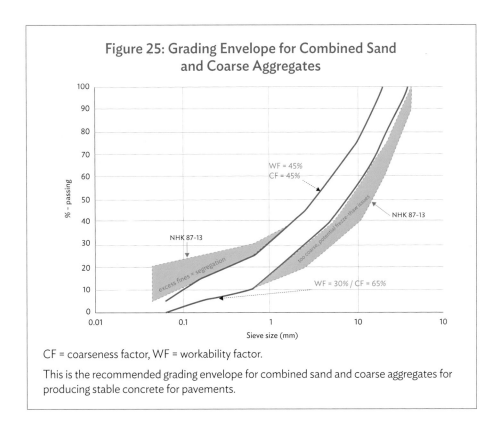

Figure 25: Grading Envelope for Combined Sand and Coarse Aggregates

CF = coarseness factor, WF = workability factor.

This is the recommended grading envelope for combined sand and coarse aggregates for producing stable concrete for pavements.

Finally, the overall combined grading of fine and coarse aggregates should not contain more than 5.0% material passing 0.063 mm (fines). The reason for this is not only related to the fact that fine particles are potentially deleterious, as shown previously, but also that fine particles add up with cement to make the volume of paste (cement + sand + water + air) in concrete.

The average content of combined aggregates in a concrete mix for pavements might be about 1,800–1,900 kg, meaning that 5.0% of this mass (90–100 kg/m³) is "fines." It is not recommended to exceed a combined mass of cement + fines of more than 480 kg/m³ in a concrete mix for pavement, to control workability, workability retention, and segregation.

Thus, the minimum cement content should be specified based on the environment the concrete will be exposed to in service and the target characteristic strength. For concrete exposed to freeze-thaw, the European standard (EN 206-1:2013) requires minimum 340 kg/m³ of cement and a water/cement ratio of 0.45 maximum in combination with a target air content of 4.0% (Chapter 3).

If 340 kg/m³ allows obtaining the *in situ* characteristic flexural strength for concrete plus margin, following the definitions given in Chapter 1, this should be the minimum specified dosage of cement with the additional requirement that the total content of fines in the mix (cement + fines) should not exceed 480 kg/m³. Cement particles, in fact, are all passing 0.063 mm and, as such, belong to the definition of fines given in this guide.

This means that if a contractor finds, for instance, 100 kg/m³ of fines in the overall aggregate and fines are not deleterious under the definitions given in Tables 12 and 13), the dosage of cement should not exceed 380 kg/m³, providing flexural strength and other prescribed properties such as free-thaw resistance can be achieved. If more cement is required, cleaner aggregates must be used.

Table 12: Entry Data of ASTM C33 Envelope for Coarse Aggregates

Sieve Size (mm)	%- passing	
40	100	100
20	100	75
10	75	55
5	60	40
2.5	45	30
1.25	35	20
0.63	25	10
0.16	15	5
0.063	5	0

Shape of aggregates dictates how workable, strong, and durable the resulting concrete will be. Aggregates are described by three dimensions (Figure 26). When the least dimension (A) is less than 33% of the longest dimension (C), we define the aggregate as flaky (plate-like). When the longest direction is at least 33% more than the intermediate dimension (B), the aggregate is said to be elongated.

We define an aggregate as "cubical" when the three dimensions are similar and all faces are crushed (Figure 26). We define an aggregate as "spherical" when the three dimensions are similar and all faces are round.

Figure 26: Three Dimensions of Aggregates

A - shortest or least dimension
C - longest or principal dimension
B - intermediate dimension

Crushed 20-37.5 mm aggregates. Generally cubical in shape with some elongated and flaky particles.

River gravel. A sample of round spherical coarse aggregate.

Aggregates (fine and coarse) quarried from rivers with no further mechanical processing except for sieving are generally round. They favor concrete workability but they do not favor flexural strength for instance, due to the lower bonding with cement paste.

Crushed aggregates (fine and coarse) do not favor workability when the amount of flaky and elongated particles exceeds 33% of the total grains respectively, but they favor flexural strength (when the quantity of flaky particles is less than 35%) because of the increased bond between paste and aggregate, and because of the higher surface area.

In general, it is recommended to use 100% crushed coarse aggregates for concrete pavements because of the better resistance to abrasion and increased skid resistance provided by fractured faces versus rounded ones.

Chloride-free sand for pavements can either originate from natural sources (rivers or lakes, providing grading is suitable and deleterious materials minimized), or from crushing or, finally, from a combination of these two sources.

Sand with FM of less than 2.4 (some river sand and all of the desert dune sand) should not be used alone to manufacture concrete for pavements unless blended with coarse crushed sand. Sand with an FM in excess of 3.4 is expected to be too coarse. A list of tests and limits for flakiness of aggregates is given in Table 13.

D. Specifications for Aggregates

Based on all what has been discussed in this chapter, the following parameters should be controlled, evaluated, and tested when assessing the suitability of fine and coarse aggregates for concrete paving, especially when a new quarry is being developed for a specific project (Tables 12, 13). The geological assessment of the aggregates is, however, the preliminary step in this process because, as we have seen, most of the properties of the resulting concrete depend on the aggregates geology.

Flaky particles. The effect of flaky particles in a segregating concrete mix.

Table 13: Coarse Aggregates Specifications

Test	United States	Europe	Suggested Maximum Limits for Concrete for Pavements
Petrographic analysis	ASTM C295	EN 932-3	Define hazardous minerals for alkali reactions, frost attack, etc.
Clay lumps and friable particles	ASTM C142	–	5%
Chert (less than 2.40 specific gravity)	ASTM C123	–	5%
Sum of clay lumps, friable particles, and chert (less than 2.40 specific gravity)	–	–	7%
Material finer than 0.063 mm	–	EN 932-1	1.5%
Coal and lignite	ASTM C123	–	0.5%
Flakiness and elongation index	ASTM D4791	EN 933-4	35%
Magnesium sulfate soundness (5 cycles)	ASTM C88	–	18%
Magnesium sulfate soundness	–	EN 1367-2	
Los Angeles abrasion	ASTM C131	EN 1097-2	40% (determined on the fraction 10–20 mm) (lower it to 30% for concrete exposed to severe freeze-thaw)
Acid-soluble sulfate	–	EN 1744-5	0.8%
Water absorption	ASTM C127	EN 1097-6	4% (lower it to 2% for concrete exposed to severe freeze-thaw)

mm = millimeter.

These limits are taken from international experience with well-performing concrete pavements in service constructed with limits like (or similar to) the ones below. Options for testing standards are given according to ASTM and EN, when applicable.

The maximum aggregate size should be limited to 20 mm for concrete exposed to severe freeze-thaw attack unless aggregates are proven to be non-frost-susceptible.

Also, for concrete exposed to severe freeze-thaw, coarse aggregates should not have more than 2% absorption.

Fines content (% passing 0.063 mm) should be limited to:

(i)   7% in sand,
(ii)   1.5 % in coarse aggregates,
(iii) 5% in the combined grading.

Table 14: Fine Aggregates Specifications

Test	United States	Europe	Suggested Max Limits For Concrete For Pavements
Petrographic analysis	ASTM C295	EN 932-3	Define hazardous minerals for alkali reactions, frost attack, etc.
Clay lumps and friable particles	ASTM C142	–	3%
Organic impurities	ASTM C40	–	Equal or lighter than standard color
Chert less than 2.40 SG	ASTM	–	5%
Sum of clay lumps, friable particles and chert (less than 2.40 SG)	ASTM C 142	–	7%
Material finer than 0.063 mm	–	EN 932-1	3% (natural sand) 10% (crushed sand)
Coal and lignite	ASTM C123	–	1%
Magnesium sulfate soundness (5 cycles)	ASTM C88	–	15%
Magnesium sulfate soundness		EN 1367-2	
Acid soluble sulfate		EN 1744-5	0.8%

mm = millimeter, SG = specific gravity.

3

Production of Concrete for Rigid Pavements

A. Introduction and Overview

Concrete for rigid pavements contains the same basic components of structural concrete: cement, aggregates, water, and chemical admixtures. These components are used to reduce water content, to control setting, and to enhance resistance to freeze and thaw, among other properties.

However, the way components are proportioned in concrete for pavements at the mix design stage is not entirely similar to how other types of concrete are proportioned. Jointed plain concrete pavements (JPCPs) rely greatly on how the mix design is developed to ensure volumetric stability, tensile strength, and mechanical and environmental durability.

Unlike reinforced concrete, where steel controls how wide and spaced cracks are and in which the steel absorbs tensile stresses, JPCPs rely on saw cuts for defining crack spacing, while the opening of cracks depends on drying shrinkage, and the coefficient of thermal expansion of aggregates, as we have seen in Chapter 1.

The most important parameters to be considered and controlled when designing concrete mixes for rigid pavements are:

(i)   workability,
(ii)   workability retention,
(iii)   initial and final setting time,
(iv)   air content,
(v)   water content,
(vi)   resistance to segregation,
(vii)   aggregates types and proportions,
(viii) cement content and type,
(ix)   target flexural strength, and
(x)   durability.

It is beyond the scope of this handbook to provide guidance on the influence of cement content and type on strength and durability. Some basic rules for proportioning aggregates and cement have been defined in Chapter 2. How durability is greatly affected by aggregates type and size have been extensively discussed.

The influence of other parameters on the final product—such as workability, setting time, dosage, and type of chemical admixtures, as well as water content of aggregates and concrete—will be discussed in the ensuing section.

B. Workability

Workability is a measure of how fresh concrete can consolidate under an applied external force (gravity or vibration). One of the most common and simple workability tests widely used for concrete for pavements is the Abram's cone test, also known as the slump cone test (Figure 27).

Figure 27: Slump Cone Test

  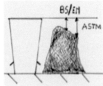

1. The cone is filled with concrete in three equal layers, and each is compacted with 25 tamps of the tamping

2. The cone is lowly raised and the concrete is allowed to slump under its own weight

3. The slump is measured using the upturned cone and slump rod as a guide. BS/EN measure slump in center.
ASTM on the lower point.

Slump apparatus. This apparatus is in accordance with EN 12350-2 and ASTM C 143 (photo via www.matest.com).

Slump value. The slump value is the difference between the height of the metal cone and the height of concrete after flowing under gravity and coming to rest.

The slump value is the difference between the height of the metal cone and the height of concrete after flowing under gravity and coming to rest. The European standard for the production of concrete (British Standards Institute 2021) defines five classes of slump (Table 15).

Table 15: Slump Test by Class

Class	Slump Tested in Accordance with EN 12350-2
S1	10 to 40 mm
S2	50 to 90 mm
S3	100 to 150 mm
S4	160 to 210 mm
S5	>220 mm

Keeping all other factors constant, higher slump is obtained by increasing the dosage of water or, by keeping the water content constant and using chemical admixtures, to enhance workability. As increasing water causes mechanical properties and durability to be reduced, modern concrete minimizes the content of water and maximizes the content of chemical admixtures.

Concrete for fixed-form paving, (i.e., where fixed and rigid side forms are used to control the verticality of edges, Figure 28) is usually cast in S2 class, while concrete for slipform (i.e., where verticality of edges is controlled only by the stability of concrete formed by the moving forms of the slipform paver, Figure 28) is cast in S1 class. Very low slump is required for slipform to control "edge slump," which is the plastic collapse of the side of the slab after the moving forms are past.

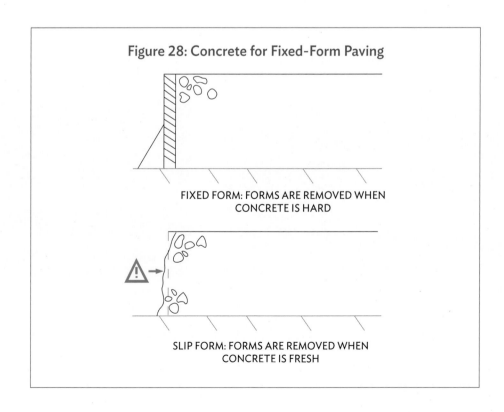

Figure 28: Concrete for Fixed-Form Paving

FIXED FORM: FORMS ARE REMOVED WHEN
CONCRETE IS HARD

SLIP FORM: FORMS ARE REMOVED WHEN
CONCRETE IS FRESH

For slipform concrete, the usual practical target value of slump is defined as ranging between 20 mm and 30 mm. When target values are used instead of the ranges of Table 14, the tolerances set by EN 206-1: 2013 depend on the value of the target.

For target values of less than 40 mm, the tolerance is ±10 mm, while for target values between 50 mm and 90 mm, the tolerance is ±20 mm. If, for instance, field tests prove that 25 mm is the target slump for controlling edge slump in a job site with slipform paving, the range of acceptance for slump values in the project should be 15 ÷ 35 mm.

Acceptable workability for slipform and fixed-form means the workability that concrete must have at placing. However, initial concrete workability at the point of production is generally higher than the workability at the point of delivery.

Workability Retention

The rate at which workability decreases after batching is a function of:

(i)   ambient temperature (the higher the temperature, the greater the workability loss);
(ii)   wind speed and humidity (the larger the wind speed and the lower the humidity, the greater the workability loss);
(iii)   concrete temperature (the higher the temperature, the greater the workability loss);
(iv)   initial slump (the higher the slump, the lower the workability loss with time);
(v)   aggregates absorption (the higher the absorption, the greater the workability loss);
(vi)   cement (dosage, type, grade, fineness);
(vii)   distance (the longer the distance between production and placement, the greater the workability loss); and
(viii) chemical admixture dosage and type.

There are no fixed rules to predict how fast workability will decrease, since the variables are many and change from place to place. To determine the workability loss, trials at the production plant should be carried out, where concrete is batched and workability is measured after discharge, where it is measured again at 30' intervals or less, as required.

If workability loss is assessed in summer, a new assessment for winter shall be required and vice versa. Once the rate of workability loss is determined, it is possible to estimate at which initial slump concrete must be produced to be delivered at the point of destination within the acceptable limits for optimal placing.

Figure 29 shows an example of optimization of workability retention for a concrete mix. Four options are compared with the slump value measured at intervals of time calculated from first addition of water to cement. Target onsite is 30 mm at 90' from first addition of water.

Mix A has unacceptable workability loss within 60', mix B has excessive slump of 80 mm at 90', mix C has 30 mm slump at 75', while mix D has 30 mm at 110'. Hence, the optimal choice for the job site is a mix in between C and D.

To control workability and to replicate the behavior of concrete from batch to batch, water-reducing admixtures and retarding admixtures are always used in modern concrete for pavements.

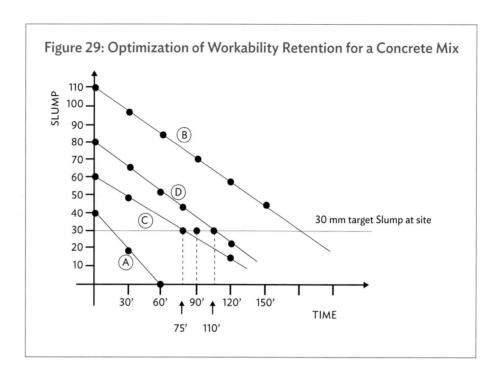

Figure 29: Optimization of Workability Retention for a Concrete Mix

Plasticizers, Superplasticizers, and Retarders

Plasticizers, superplasticizers, and retarders are chemical admixtures for concrete. One of the most comprehensive specification for admixtures for concrete is ASTM International 2017b. The admixtures of interest for concrete workability are:

(i)   Type A: water reducing admixtures;
(ii)   Type B: retarding;
(iii) Type D: water reducing and retarding;
(iv)   Type F: water reducing, high range; and
(v)   Type G: water reducing, high range, and retarding.

Type A, B, D (also known as plasticizers) must allow a reduction of at least 5% in the water content for the same workability.

Thus, for instance, if the slump of concrete without a type A, B, D admixture is 100 mm with 200 kilograms/cubic meter (kg/m³) of water and a water/cement ratio of 0.50, the addition of one of these admixtures should allow a reduction of 10 kg of water per m³ and the water/cement ratio would decrease to 0.48 but slump would remain 100 mm. Type A, B, D admixtures belong to the chemical category of lignosulphonates.

Type F, G admixtures (also known as superplasticizers) must allow a reduction of at least 12% in the water content for the same workability. For the above example we calculate a minimum reduction of water of 24 kg/m³ and the water/cement ratio is lowered further down to 0.44 while slump remains 100 mm. Type F, G admixtures are synthetic polymers.

However, the reality in modern day concrete technology is that Type A and D admixtures allow up to 15% reduction in water content, while type F and G allow up to 30% or more.

All of these admixtures consist of a dispersion of active solids (up to 40% by mass) in water. For a given chemical composition (naphthalene or polymer), the higher the content of solids, the more effective the dispersion is in terms of water reduction and/or, when applicable, retardation.

The advantage of type A, D admixtures is that they are generally cheaper and maintain the concrete cohesive (less prone to segregation) even at high dosage. The disadvantage of type A, D admixtures is that they require very high dosage (generally from 1.5% to 2.0% by mass of cement) and they can promote, if overdosed, strong retardation in the setting of concrete, which is not something any concrete pavement should experience to avoid early cracking.

Type B admixtures are not recommended to be used alone for concrete pavements, because they act as very strong retarders that can cause severe delay in setting, followed by uncontrolled cracking. Type B admixtures are sometimes used in combination with types A or D when extended workability is required for long transport times and/or very hot weather.

Type F and type G admixtures are generally dosed from 0.5% to 1.8% by mass of cement but, depending on the polymer and water reduction capacity, they are more expensive than lignosulphonate ones. The advantage of type F and G admixtures is that they allow to batch concrete, which is stronger and more durable, because of the reduced water/m3 required to obtain a certain workability and workability retention.

However, for mixes with a relatively low content of fines as defined in Chapter 2, they might promote segregation if water content of aggregates in the plant is not properly controlled.

Concrete mix comparison. Comparison between a concrete mix produced with a water and cement ratio of 0.40 with 1.6% of type F admixture (left) and the same concrete mix produced with a water–cement ratio of 0.47 and the same amount of admixture (right). The increase in water for the same dosage of admixture has caused the concrete to segregate.

The rules of thumb for concrete technology applied to pavements when it comes to the choice of admixture are:

(i)   avoid using type B retarding admixtures alone as they may promote strong delay in setting time;
(ii)   use a type F superplasticizer alone for cold weather, as lower temperature helps workability retention;
(iii)   use a type F superplasticizer for hot weather to control workability and, if necessary, combine it with a type A, D plasticizer/ retarder to control setting time for long transport; and
(iv)   use type G admixtures only when the combined fines from cement and aggregates as defined in Chapter 2 exceeds 430 kg/m^3.

In general, the optimization of the dosage and type of admixtures is made with laboratory and plant trials mocking the production of concrete until the following parameters have been reached satisfactorily:

(i)   workability,
(ii)   workability retention, and
(iii)   controlled setting time.

C. Voids Content of Concrete

When a concrete surface is exposed to water from rain, it will absorb some of it. Although, to the naked eye concrete might seem very compact and massive, at the microscopic scale it contains several tiny cracks with width from few tens to few hundreds of millimeters only.

These cracks do not cause issues for strength given their very limited width, but they can be an issue for durability because water can saturate these cracks and expand in the winter when temperature drops below freezing.

The photo shows a section of concrete analyzed under a microscope using an optical enhancing technique for detecting cracks and pores named fluorescence (the scale of the image is provided in the bottom right corner) of the image.

Cracks (red arrows) appear as linear bright colored features crossing the matrix and surrounding some aggregates (darker shapes), while bright pores can be spherical or, more commonly, irregularly shaped with dimensions from a few tens of millimeters up to a few millimeters such as the case of the pore circled in yellow.

Capillary cracks are inevitable in concrete and form as a result of hydration and mainly poor curing, while pores are made out of air naturally entrapped during the process of batching, transporting, and placing. Capillary cracks and pores together form the voids system of the concrete.

Because capillary cracks and voids are interconnected, they form a network of discontinuities where water and other fluids permeating from the surface can accumulate.

As the width of these features is very narrow, when water is trapped within them and it expands under frost conditions, it will create extremely high pressures of up to several MPa that can locally exceed the tensile strength of the matrix and cause breakage. This is the phenomenon called scaling which is typical of concrete surfaces exposed cyclically to freeze and thaw.

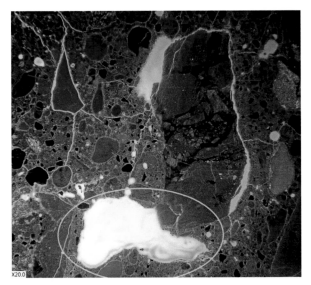

Analysis. Concrete section analyzed under a microscope.

Freeze and thaw. Example of scaling from the surface of a concrete pavement.

The total number of capillary cracks depends mainly, keeping other factors constant, from the initial water content of the mix. Generally, only about 25% of water expressed as mass of cement is required to generate a fully hydrated paste. This corresponds to a water–cement (W/C) ratio of 0.25. In this case, all water is used to hydrate the cement.

Thus, to fully hydrate 380 kg of cement (which is one common dosage of cement per cubic meter for concrete for pavements) only about 95 kg of water is sufficient. However, with such low quantity of water, unless an extremely high (thus uneconomical) dosage of plasticizer or superplasticizer is used, concrete would be too dry. Hence, more water must be added to reduce the cost of admixture and obtain the required consistency.

When water is in excess of 25% of the mass of cement it will not all react with cement grains and part of it can be lost by evaporation (evaporable water) when concrete is hardened. The loss of water by evaporation leaves behind a network of capillary cracks. The higher the W/C ratio, the higher the number of cracks, and the higher the absorption of concrete in service will be, and, finally, the lower the resistance to freeze-thaw of the pavement.

Since entrapped air pores in concrete account only for about 2% by volume (or 20 liters over 1,000 liters of concrete produced), and since durable concrete mixes with W/C ratio of 0.40 contain about 14%–16% of total voids as testing experience shows, the volume of capillary cracks in concrete can easily be of about 12%–14% (or 120–140 liters over 1,000 liters), which is a considerable amount.

To reduce this volume, W/C ratio must be lowered as much as possible, but experience shows that 10%–2% is the minimum volume of total voids in a concrete mix, of which about 8%–10% is, therefore, made out capillary cracks, or 80 to 100 liters of voids over 1,000 liters of concrete produced.

To further reduce the volume of capillary cracks, high dosage of the so-called supplementary cementitious materials can be used (fly ash, ground granulated blast-furnace slag, metakaolin, silica fume, etc.). These compounds are known to consume calcium hydroxide available in the concrete paste from the hydration of the clinker present in the cement and they produce new crystals of calcium-silicate hydrates that seal some of the capillary cracks through pozzolanic reactions.

Some special admixtures that work to reduce concrete permeability (called hydrophilic or hydrophobic admixtures) may be used as well.

However, for concrete pavements the amount of supplementary cementitious materials is limited to dosages that do not affect workability, setting time and plastic shrinkage cracking and such dosages (usually not more than 20%–25% replacement of cement by weight at best) are generally not effective in creating the complete sealing of capillary cracks. The use of specific admixtures to lower permeability may be, finally, uneconomical.

Significant consideration should be given to curing (Chapter 5). If a moist environment is provided at the surface of the concrete pavement in the first days after casting, water remains in the capillary cracks as the rate of evaporation will be reduced dramatically.

When the concrete is hardened, some of this water will react with carbon dioxide and with calcium hydroxide present along the cracks' walls in the concrete matrix and form crystals of calcium carbonate that block cracks.

This is known as natural self-healing and it is the reason why well-cured concrete is less permeable, hence more durable, because, due to natural self-healing, some of the water in the voids is combined to form calcium carbonate.

Air Entrainers for Concrete

The strategy to control and enhance concrete durability against scaling is to provide artificial air entraining in the concrete at the time of batching.

Air-entraining admixtures (conforming to ASTM International 2010) produce, depending on the dosage, a controlled volume of entrained air bubbles, which are spherical in shape and of smaller size than entrapped air, which is incorporated during the process of mixing.

Experience teaches that when there is 3.0%–6.0% of air entrained in concrete, there is a dramatic improvement in freeze-thaw resistance of the paste. Air bubbles created by these admixtures range in size from about 0.1 mm to 1.0 mm and they can be in a number ranging from 10,000–100,000 dispersed in the concrete volume. The beneficial effect of these bubbles is to work as pressure relief for the expansion of the cement paste when water in capillary cracks freezes and expands.

The main disadvantage of air-entrainers is that it is generally difficult to control the target air content within narrow limits. Seasonal changes in temperature, changes in the fines content of aggregates and in the cement type and fineness can all influence the amount of air entrained for the same dosage of admixture. Thus, a certain dosage working in a certain period of time may not give the same result in another period.

Also, for each 1% increase in entrained air, there is roughly about 3%–5% decrease in compressive strength. Hence, when designing concrete mixes containing artificially entrained air this must be considered.

It is important therefore to control air content of the concrete frequently during the day, to adjust for variations that can impact durability (insufficient air content) and strength (excessive air content). Air content of concrete is measured in the field with the portable and inexpensive apparatus as shown in the photo.

Air content apparatus. An example of the air content apparatus
(ASTM Intl. n.d.; British Standards Institution 2019b)
(Photo: www.controls.com).

Finally, when concrete is transported for long durations, the air content might be partially lost at the point of arrival, requiring the producer to account for this loss by batching concrete with a higher air content than the target on site.

Because the dosage of air-entrainers is very low, usually from 0.1%–0.5% by mass of cement it may also be difficult to dose them in small volume batches.

If, for instance, a 1.0 m³ batch of concrete contains 400 kg of cement and the air entrainer is dosed at 0.2%, only 0.8 kg of admixture is required, which might be not precisely dosed by the dispensing system due to the very small mass involved.

If 3.0 m³ are produced at the same time, the amount of admixture would be 2.4 kg/m³ and the error of the dispensing system would reduce.

Sometimes manufacturers of air-entrainers produce diluted versions that allow higher dosage. In the above example, if the 0.1% of concentrated air entrainer is replaced by, say, 0.5% of the diluted version (five times diluted), the result may not change in terms of admixture's efficiency, but 1.0m3 of concrete would now require 3.0 kg/m³ of admixture and 3.0 m³ would require 9.0 kg/m³, with a strong reduction in potential weighing errors.

The recommended target content of air at the delivery point when concrete pavements are exposed to freeze-thaw is: 4.0 ± 1.5%.

D. Initial and Final Setting Time

When water is added to cement, hydration begins, which ultimately leads to the formation of a hardened structure with a strength, i.e., an ability to resist external loads.

When concrete is freshly batched, it behaves like a viscous fluid in the sense that it spreads under its own weight, as the slump test is designed to show. Concrete flows because of the potential energy stored in the slump cone's center of gravity. Hence, when the slump cone is lifted up concrete will collapse and it will flow laterally, transforming potential energy into kinetic energy until it will reach an equilibrium between residual potential energy, internal friction, and friction with the base.

If after 30' the slump test is repeated, the concrete can still flow, but equilibrium is reached before the spread is complete as if some internal force acts to prevent further movement. At this stage there is internal cohesion opposing the flow. To spread the concrete further down, external effort (vibrator, shocks etc.) will need to be added. Concrete is still workable but it also has increased internal cohesion due to the ongoing hydration processes. This effect can be observed in the second, third, and fourth images.

In one of the images presented below, the concrete is still workable (hence, slump is greater than 0 mm), but it also has an increased internal cohesion due to the progression of the process of hydration. At this stage, if fresh concrete is forced to flow further it will break in chunks.

The loss of workability with time is an indication of the fact that concrete undergoes setting which is caused by the interaction of water and cement particles. When water and cement come into contact thousands of needle-like crystals and other amorphous gels form, bonding cement particles together and increase internal cohesion with time.

Concrete setting time. Development of needle-like crystals in the concrete paste after 3 hours from batching (top). After 8 hours from batching, the needle-like crystals have become much more abundant (bottom).

In the early stages (generally only up to 2–3 hours from batching), workability measured with the slump cone decreases from its initial value to zero (pseudo-plastic state). When workability is zero, gravity is not enough to overcome the internal cohesion of the concrete and an external force is required (vibration). If vibration causes concrete to crack and break, concrete enters in a plastic state.

This is the final setting time, beginning with the development of internal heat, produced by the exothermic reactions of hydration of cement with water, and ending with the development of mechanical strength.

The determination of initial and final setting time of concrete can be tested in the field using the ASTM International 2017a method. Values obtained with this method can be used only for comparative purposes between different options (different versions of the same mix with different amounts of plasticizer, superplasticizer, and retarder), but they generally do not reflect the actual setting time of concrete *in situ* because of the scale effect between the sample used for testing (few kg of concrete sieved to the 4.75 mm only) and concrete in the pavement.

The knowledge of initial and final setting time of concrete for pavements is essential in planning the joints' saw-cut time.

Hydration processes. The photos here show increased internal cohesion due to ongoing hydration processes.

E. Water Content of Concrete

Concrete mixes are proportioned in a such a way that the sum of the volumes occupied by each component totals 1.0 m³ (or 1,000 liters). Because the volume V of a component can be expressed in terms of its mass M (in kg) and density δ (in kg/m³) as: $V = \dfrac{M}{\delta}$, for a concrete mix containing n components we can write:

$$\sum_{i=1}^{i=n} \frac{Mi}{\delta i} = 1.0 \text{ (cubic meter)}$$

Another important rule in proportioning concrete mixes is that all components (except water and chemical admixtures) are assumed to be dry (for aggregates, surface dry).

Finally, the ratio between the mass of water added to the concrete mix and the mass of cement is defined as: water–cement (W/C) ratio.

For any given age of concrete the general rule is that compressive strength decreases with an increase of the W/C ratio. This is known as Abrams' law. Experience teaches that for every 0.1 increase in the W/C ratio, strength is decreased by about 5%.

Also, increasing water content of concrete decreases durability as the network of capillary cracks and absorption of concrete increase, allowing water and aggressive fluids (chloride for instance) to be trapped in the concrete matrix.

Depending on the concrete exposure in service, W/C ratio should be lower than certain maximum values. Generally, for concrete exposed to freeze-thaw, concrete should be batched with a maximum water/cement ratio of 0.45 according to EN 206-1:2013 standard.

W/C ratio for concrete pavements, especially when slump must be very low (slipform placement), it is usually between 0.35– 0.40.

Water Content of Aggregates

When producing concrete from a plant, one main problem is that aggregates are rarely dry. Because of quarrying operations or exposure to rain or snow, aggregates are generally wet. The ideal bone-dry state for an aggregate is reached when it is dried in the oven for 24 hours at 105°C.

If the aggregate is soaked in water for 24 hours, it will absorb some of it. The amount of absorbed water depends on the amount of voids the aggregate contains.

When an aggregate has been saturated, it has absorbed the maximum amount of water to fill its voids. The aggregate is now said to be in saturated-surface-dry condition (SSD). Any extra water added to the aggregate will now be seen as surface moisture and it will coat the surface of the aggregate as a translucent film.

When an aggregate in SSD condition is dried in the oven, there will be a difference between the initial mass before drying and the mass after drying. This difference is the absorbed water. The ratio between absorbed water and the mass of dry aggregate is defined as absorption.

$$absorption \% = \frac{(mass\ of\ SSD\ aggregate\ -\ mass\ of\ oven\ dry\ aggregate}{mass\ of\ oven\ dry\ aggregate}$$

When a wet aggregate is dried in the oven there, will be a difference between the initial mass before drying and the mass after drying. This difference is the total water content. The ratio between total water content and the mass of dry aggregate is defined as moisture content.

$$moisture\ content\ \% = \frac{(mass\ of\ WET\ aggregate - mass\ of\ oven\ dry\ aggregate)}{mass\ of\ oven\ dry\ aggregate}$$

Moisture content is always greater than absorption, because if water coats the aggregate, it means that the aggregate is also pre-saturated and the process of drying will remove both surface water and absorbed water. Figure 30 sketches the different moisture states of an aggregate particle.

By knowing absorption and moisture content of aggregates through simple laboratory tests (Tables 12 and 13) the necessary corrections to the mass of SSD aggregates used in a concrete mix design can be made. These corrections are important because the difference between absorbed water and moisture content is the free water coating the aggregates, which adds up to the water content of concrete.

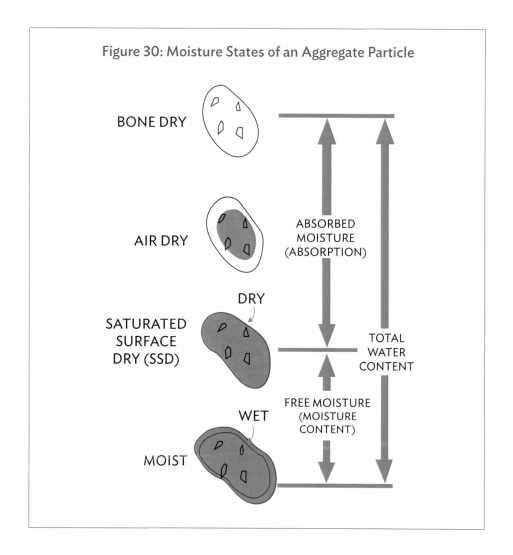

Figure 30: Moisture States of an Aggregate Particle

Surface dry condition. Sample of aggregate particles subjected to surface dry condition or SDD.

Water content. Sample of wet aggregate particles.

Water Correction in Concrete Production

Table 16 shows the proportion of concrete mix.

The mix design in Table 15 is proportioned to have a so-called yield of 1.00 m³ and a unit weight of concrete of 2,482 kg/m³. The W/C ratio is set at 0.40. It also incorporates 4.0% (or 40 liters over 1,000 liters) of entrained air provided by an air-entraining admixture dosed at 1.14 kg/m³ (or 0.3% by mass of cement). Sand and coarse aggregates are assumed to be in SSD condition.

The free moisture of aggregates can be calculated from the difference between moisture content and absorption, then the product between columns **a** and **d** of Table 16 is the free water in the aggregates. It is called free because it is available for the mixing process of concrete, unlike absorbed water which is not available, being trapped in the voids of the aggregate.

Table 16: Proportion of Concrete Mix

Component	Mass (kg)	Density (kg/m³)	Volume (m³)	Moisture Content (%)	Absorption (%)
Cement	380	3,100	0.1226		
Sand (SSD)	750	2,700	0.2778	5.00%	1.50%
5-10 mm (SSD)	450	2,700	0.1667	2.50%	1.00%
10-20 mm (SSD)	745	2,700	0.2759	1.50%	1.00%
Water	152	1,000	0.1520		
Plasticizer	3.8	1,180	0.0032		
Air entrainer	1.14	1,050	0.0011		
Air content	--	--	0.04		
Unit Weight*	**2,482 kg/m³**	**Volume**	**1.00 m³**		

SSD = saturated-surface-dry, mm = millimeter, kg = kilogram, kg/m³ = kilogram per cubic meter.

*Sum of the masses of components used to produce 1.0 m³.

Table 17: Free Moisture of Aggregates Calculation

	a	b	c	d	e
	Mass SSD (kg)	Moisture Content	Absorption	Free Moisture	Free Water (kg)
Sand	750	5.00%	1.50%	3.50%	26.3
5-10 mm	450	2.50%	1.00%	1.50%	6.8
10-20 mm	745	1.50%	1.00%	0.50%	3.7

ABS = absorption, kg = kilogram, MC = moisture content, mm = millimeter, SSD = saturated-surface-dry.

From Table 17, we realize that if we desire the mass of aggregates to be as designed, there are two corrections to be made to account for their free moisture. The first one considers that water has a mass, hence wet aggregates are heavier than dry aggregates, and the second one considers that, if aggregates add free water in the mix, the W/C ratio will increase. This process is done in Table 17 where values in column **f** are obtained by summing values in column a with values in column **e**.

From Table 18 we notice that aggregates add a total of 36.7 kg of water in the mix (sum of rows of column **e**).

Table 18: Wet Mass Calculation

	a	f	b	c	d	e
	Mass SSD (kg)	Mass (WET) (kg)	Moisture Content	Absorption	Free Moisture	Free Water (kg)
Sand	750	776.3	5.00%	1.50%	3.50%	26.3
5-10 mm	450	456.8	2.50%	1.00%	1.50%	6.8
10-20 mm	745	748.7	1.50%	1.00%	0.50%	3.7

ABS = absorption, kg = kilogram, MC = moisture content, mm = millimeter, SSD = saturated-surface-dry.

The total water content of the mix now becomes, from Tables 14 and 16, 188.7 kg and the new W/C ratio is 0.50. Because for every 0.01 point of W/C ratio strength reduces by roughly 5%, we conclude that the expected strength of the mix has decreased by roughly 50%.

Therefore, to account for the free water added to the mix by aggregates, the free moisture of aggregates must be subtracted from the water content of the mix to keep the W/C ratio constant. Table 19 shows the correction for water made to maintain the W/C ratio constant at 0.40, which was the original target value set in this example.

This process, when concrete is produced by a batching plant, is usually automatically performed by the software that manages the system.

The mix design of Table 19 is converted into a "batch report" similar to that in Table 20. The software adjusts the weight of aggregates based on the free moisture and it subtracts the free water added by the aggregates from the target water, to keep the W/C ratio constant.

Hence, controlling moisture content and absorption of aggregates is of paramount importance to produce consistent concrete with the target W/C ratio, strength, durability, and workability. The next section will discuss the systems for controlling moisture content of concrete in the batching plant.

Table 19: Correction for Water Made to Maintain the Water–Cement Ratio Constant at 0.40

Component	Mass (kg)	Density (kg/m³)	Volume (m³)
Cement	380	3100	0.1226
Sand (SSD)	750	2700	0.2778
5-10 mm (SSD)	450	2700	0.1667
10-20 mm (SSD)	745	2700	0.2759
Water	115.3	1000	0.1153
Free water in aggregates	36.7	1000	0.0367
Plasticizer	3.8	1180	0.0032
Air entrainer	1.14	1050	0.0011
Air content	–	–	0.04
Unit Weight	**2482**	**Volume**	**1.00**

SSD = saturated-surface-dry, mm = millimeter, kg = kilogram, kg/m³ = kilogram per cubic meter.

Table 20: Mixed Design Conversion into a Batch Report

Component	MIX DESIGN Mass (kg)	BATCHED Mass (kg)	Moisture content	Absorption
Cement	380	380		
Sand	750	776.3	5.00%	1.50%
5-10 mm	450	456.8	2.50%	1.00%
10-20 mm	745	748.7	1.50%	1.00%
Target water	152.0	115.3		
Water in aggregates	–	36.7		
Plasticizer	3.8	3.8		
Air entrainer	1.14	1.14		

mm = millimeter, kg = kilogram, kg/m³ = kilogram per cubic meter.

Although the use of bone-dry aggregates is rare and limited only to aggregates produced and stockpiled for prolonged periods of time in arid climate, it is worth giving an example of calculations to maintain the correct W/C ratio.

Using bone-dry aggregates is equal, according to the definitions discussed above, to setting 0% moisture content in Table 18 to obtain Table 21 below.

Without a water correction in the target water of the mix of Table 19, this fraction of water (–23.2 kg) would be absorbed by the bone-dry aggregates during mixing and transport. The water content of the concrete would no longer be as designed, and this reduction might impact initial workability and workability retention as the W/C ratio is now decreased from 0.40 to only 0.34.

When using bone-dry aggregates and/or aggregates that have been stockpiled for long periods of time in dry environment this correction must be considered to prevent issues with rapid loss of workability caused by absorption of some of the target water by the aggregates. Once again, this process is usually controlled automatically by the batching plant's computer.

Table 21: Sample Calculations to Maintain the Correct Water–Cement Ratio

	Mass SSD (kg)	Moisture Content	Absorption	ABS Water (kg)
Sand	750	0.00%	1.50%	-11.3
5-10 mm	450	0.00%	1.00%	-4.5
10-20 mm	745	0.00%	1.00%	-7.5

ABS = absorption, MC = moisture content, SSD = saturated-surface-dry, mm = millimeter, kg = kilogram.

F. Management of Concrete Production

Concrete for pavements can only be produced by automatic batching plants given the strict requirements for workability, strength, and durability. A sketch of a typical batching plant's layout is given in Figure 31.

As for any industrial process, the quality of the output of a concrete plant depends largely on the quality of the input (quality of components), and because aggregates make about 70%–80% of the volume of concrete for pavements, they play a major role in the quality of the final product.

Chapter 2 showed the main factors of influence for the quality of aggregates. The do's and don'ts in the management of aggregates stockpiled at the plant will be discussed, followed by indications on proper management of admixtures, temperature of concrete, and weighing systems.

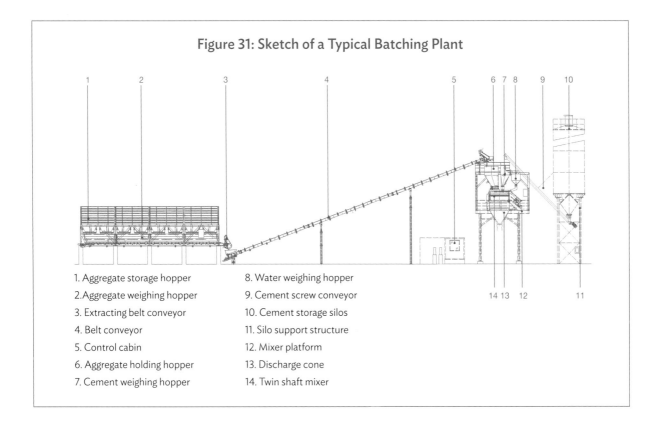

Figure 31: Sketch of a Typical Batching Plant

1. Aggregate storage hopper
2. Aggregate weighing hopper
3. Extracting belt conveyor
4. Belt conveyor
5. Control cabin
6. Aggregate holding hopper
7. Cement weighing hopper
8. Water weighing hopper
9. Cement screw conveyor
10. Cement storage silos
11. Silo support structure
12. Mixer platform
13. Discharge cone
14. Twin shaft mixer

Batching plants. Concrete for pavements can only be produced by automatic batching plants given the strict requirements for workability, strength, and durability.

Aggregates Management

The main issues to be considered when addressing the management of aggregates at the concrete plant refer to water content and segregation. Natural sand, quarried from river beds or lakes, tend to be very wet, sometimes with moisture content of up to 15%. Using very wet sand may lead to severe problems with the resulting concrete. If sand is excessively wet, the batching plant's dispensing system for the water may not start at all.

Consider a concrete mix design containing 800 kg/m³ of natural sand delivered with 15% free moisture content. As discussed previously, the water added by sand is 90 kg/m³.

Coarse aggregates are also usually moist and add even more water—assuming 1,000 kg/m³ of coarse aggregates with a moisture content of, for example, 4%, will add some more 40 kg/m³ of water from coarse aggregates.

The total water from aggregates (fine and coarse) is 130 kg/m³ and the typical water content for a durable concrete mix for pavements does not exceed generally 150 kg/m³.

This means, in this example, that the computer will adjust the target water to add 20 kg/m³ only to maintain the W/C ratio constant, creating an alarm in the system that will halt the process, because of insufficient water dosed by weighing hopper.(element 8 of Figure 31).

Second, using very wet sand leads to accumulation of water at the bottom of the aggregate hopper (element 1) which is transported, undetected, on the belt (element 4) into the mixer (element 14), increasing dramatically the water content of concrete.

Quarry in Malaysia. A quarry for the extraction of natural sand having an extremely high moisture content.

Saturated sand. A wheel loader is used to transport saturated sand directly into the batching plant hopper.

When natural sand is used to produce concrete and when the moisture content exceeds 6%–8%, it is highly recommended to create temporary stockpiling, over a concrete slab with adequate slope, to allow drainage prior to use.

When sand is temporarily stockpiled to drain, the loading of buckets of sand shall be made only from about 0.5 m above ground to avoid loading of extremely wet material.

Crushed sand on the other side is usually delivered at no more than 5% moisture content, making it easier to manage in terms of control of water. However, crushed sand segregates as it dries specially in tall stockpiles.

Temporary stockpiling. A concrete slab with adequate slope is subject to temporary stockpiling.

If the wheel loader operator hauls crushed sand from the stockpile, without blending the upper and lower portions of the stockpile first, loads of coarse sand and fine sand will alternate in the hopper with dramatic repercussions on the consistency of the concrete being produced. Abrupt changes of grain size as concrete is being produced may lead to issues with workability and segregation.

Crushed sand segregation. Tall stockpiles of segregated crushed sand.

Coarse aggregates, because of the lower specific surface in respect to sand, usually do not create issues for the control of moisture, although when they are very wet (3% or more) they can lead to the same issues of accumulation of water in the bottom of the hopper, which is then conveyed undetected to the plant's mixer.

When very wet aggregates (fine and coarse) are expected to drain water in the hoppers, the first concrete batches of the morning (if hoppers were filled the evening before) may be extremely wet and unusable. It is always better, in these cases, to empty the hoppers and fill them with fresh and drier material before beginning the production day.

When moisture content and homogeneity of sand is under control, the next potential issue is exposure to rain or snow of fine and coarse aggregates. Also, in some particularly hot climates with dark-colored aggregates, exposure to direct sunlight can lead to an increase of the temperature of the aggregates and of the fresh concrete.

Protecting aggregates from exposure. Shading is recommended to prevent aggregates from being exposed to drastic changes in the environment.

Aggregates must also be separated from each other to minimize contamination between fractions that can lead to changes in the grading curve of the concrete mix and may have repercussions on workability and water demand of the concrete.

The sizing of the bays where aggregates are stored in shade must be planned based on the production requirements of the project to avoid accumulation of loads of aggregates unprotected from the environment.

Separation of aggregates. Separation of different kinds of aggregate minimizes contamination between fractions.

Sizing of bays. It is important to plan storage and shading of aggregates.

For a major road project, a concrete paver may lay up to 500 m linear meters/shift. If the paving width is about 5.0 m and the concrete thickness is about 0.3 m, this is about 750 m³/shift of concrete.

If a concrete mix contains about 800 kg of sand, 500 kg of 5–10 mm, and 500 kg of 10–20 mm coarse aggregates, this will correspond to a consumption of 600 tons of sand and 375 tons of 5–10 mm and 10–20 mm, respectively.

Taking the bulk density of wet sand at 1.3 tons/m³ and that one of coarse aggregates at 1.5 tons/m³ we calculate, using the elementary relationship between mass, density, and volume—460 m³ and 333 m³ respectively for sand and each of the coarse aggregate fractions.

For a maximum stockpile's height of about 5 m, the above volumes correspond to bays of 92 square meter (m²) and 67 m² area as a minimum.

The following checklist is recommended to support aggregates management:

(i)   Check that the delivered material is what was ordered.
(ii)   Check that it is being discharged into the correct location.
(iii)   Prevent discharge of any materials that are visually not conforming (extremely wet, dirty, contaminated, and oversized).
(iv)   Store materials in a way that minimizes the risk of contamination or deterioration.
(v)   Keep records of deliveries.
(vi)   Test suspect deliveries for all properties for which conformity with the relevant standard or other specification is in doubt.
(vii)   Check periodically the water content of the aggregates.

Moisture Control

The control of moisture content is critical in producing concrete mixes that are consistent in workability, strength, and durability.

The control of moisture content in modern batching plants is carried out by moisture probes placed on the inner wall of each aggregate's hopper or on the conveyor belt. This is called continuous measuring.

The technology behind these systems is beyond the scope of this handbook. It will suffice to know that they use indirect electrical or microwave methods to monitor moisture content of fine and coarse aggregates as they are extracted from the hopper to the belt, and data are sent to the computer managing production for the continuous corrections in batching weights. Figure 32 presents typical locations of microwave moisture probes.

Experience teaches that poorly maintained sensors may, especially with sand, become encrusted with time and stop recording correct values of moisture. When this happens, the concrete mixes become inconsistent.

As a confirmatory measure taken both to check moisture probes' precision and to calibrate them periodically versus the actual moisture content of aggregates, moisture content tests are also recommended in an efficient system of concrete production.

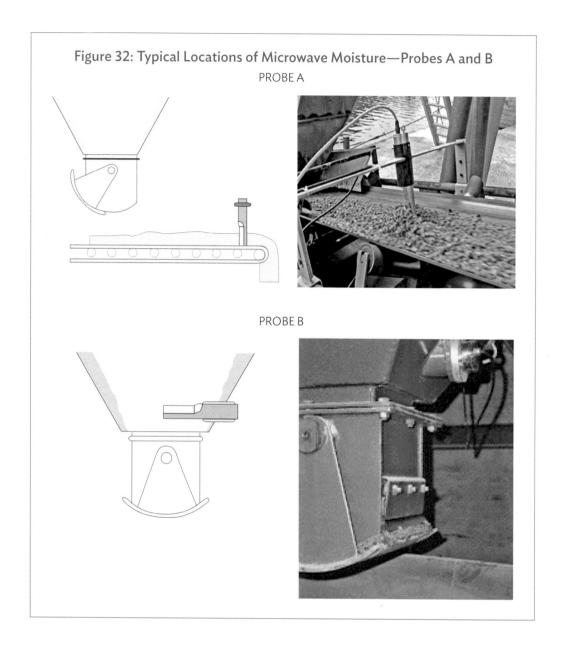

Figure 32: Typical Locations of Microwave Moisture—Probes A and B

PROBE A

PROBE B

Moisture content tests can be of two types:

(i)   oven dry (ASTM C1556); and
(ii)   speedy tests (ASTM D4944).

Oven-dry tests consist in taking a sample of aggregate and to measure the wet mass. Then the sample is dried in the oven or on a hot plate until the bone-dry condition is reached and the mass is recorded. The difference between the wet and dry mass is the water content of the aggregate, and the ratio between the water content and the dry mass of the sample is the moisture content expressed in percentage.

For the speedy moisture test, the procedure involves the reaction between water and calcium carbide which, when mixed, produce a gas. The amount of gas is directly proportional to the amount of water in the sample and results in percentage are taken from a pressure gauge.

Speedy moisture test. A pressure guage is used to determine the percentage of the amount of gas in samples of concrete mixtures (Photo: www.controls.ch).

The advantage of the speedy test is, as the name suggests, quick (few minutes) and it can be repeated many times per day. The disadvantage is that it does not provide the true moisture as the reference oven dry-test method does. However, the oven-dry method may take from 30' to a few hours for completion.

Experience shows that providing the speedy moisture test is calibrated versus the reference oven-dry method and a correlation is used, this method can be used for the daily quality control of sand moisture at the plant.

The calibration of the speedy method is as follows and it should be repeated for each sand fraction for which moisture content must be determined daily.

(i)   Take a sample of 15 kg of sand.
(ii)   Dry it in the oven for 24 hours at 105°C.
(iii)   Divide the dried mass in ten sub-samples of equal mass of 1,000 g.
(iv)   Name the samples from 1 to 10.
(v)   Add to sample 1 an amount of water equivalent to 1% of the dry mass (for instance if the dry mass is 1000 g, add 10 g) and mix it.
(vi)   Repeat the operation for samples from 2 to 10 by adding (2%, 3%, 4%...., 10% of water by dry mass of sand).

(vii)   Store each sample in a sealed bag to prevent losing any added moisture.
(viii) Split each sample into two.
(ix)   Test half of the sample for the oven-dry test (ASTM D1556).
(x)   Test the other half for speedy moisture (ASTM D4944).
(xi)   Plot the results on the graph where oven-dry results are on the x-axis and speedy results are on the y-axis.
(xii)   Make a linear regression in a spreadsheet and determine the regression equation (Figure 33).
(xiii) Use this equation to convert speedy values in oven-dry values for calibration of the moisture probes and/or water corrections at the plant.

In cases where high fluctuations of moisture content are expected on aggregates (especially sand) it is advisable to control moisture content several times during the day to monitor the amount of water in aggregates and ensure consistency of concrete.

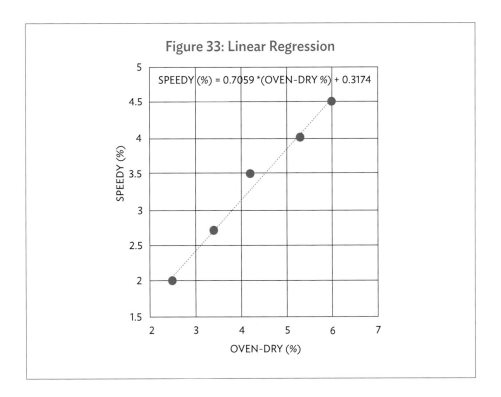

Figure 33: Linear Regression

SPEEDY (%) = 0.7059 *(OVEN-DRY %) + 0.3174

Temperature Management of Concrete

When producing concrete for pavements, it is important that, in the summer, the temperature at the delivery point does not exceed, as per international guidelines, 32°C. Excessive fresh concrete temperature can cause loss of workability and loss in ultimate strength.

The prediction of fresh concrete temperature can be made using the equation:

$$T = \frac{0.75 \cdot (M_c T_c + M_{fa} T_{fa} + M_{ca} T_{ca}) + 4.18 T_w M_w - 334 M_i}{0.75 \cdot (M_c + M_{fa} + M_{ca}) + 4.18 \cdot (M_w + M_i)} \text{ -eq 10}$$

Where:

(i)   *T* – temperature of components
(ii) *M* – Mass of components
(iii) *fa, ca, w, i* – fine aggregate, coarse aggregate, cement, water, ice (if used)

In summer conditions in continental or arid climate, freshly produced and delivered cement may have a temperature as high as 70°C, while dark coarse aggregates left in the sun may reach 35°C. Sand is usually cooler, being washed and less heat absorbent (25°C), and water is usually from ground wells, so its temperature can be taken as 25°C.

Because cement and aggregates make up most of the volume of concrete, fresh concrete temperature strongly depends on the temperature of these components. Water does not influence much temperature, unless it is cooled down with special chillers to about 5°C and/or replaced by ice flakes.

A concrete mix design with 380 kg cement, 150 kg water, 800 kg sand, and 1,000 kg coarse aggregates cast with components at the above temperatures would have an initial temperature of 34°C as calculated in Table 22 (A) using equation 10 above.

This value is generally not acceptable also in consideration that in the summer concrete gains heat while being transported. For about 30' transport time there is a further increase of 2°C–3°C making the expected fresh concrete temperature at the delivery point not to be less than 36°C–37°C.

Table 22 (B) also shows that, when cement temperature is not more than 60°C and coarse aggregates are shaded (25°C), fresh concrete temperature is lowered to 29°C. The same effect is reached when all components are at the temperatures in Table 22 (B), but water is chilled at a temperature of 5°C (table 21C).

Table 22: Comparison of Temperatures of Concrete

A		B		C	
Tc	70°C	Tc	60°C	Tc	70°C
Mc	380kg	Mc	380kg	Mc	380kg
Tfa	25°C	Tfa	25°C	Tfa	25°C
Mfa	800kg	Mfa	800kg	Mfa	800kg
Tca	35°C	Tca	25°C	Tca	35°C
Mca	1000kg	Mca	1000kg	Mca	1000kg
Tw	25°C	Tw	25°C	Tw	5°C
Mw	150kg	Mw	150kg	Mw	150kg
Mi	0kg	Mi	0kg	Mi	0kg
T	**34°C**	**T**	**29°C**	**T**	**28°C**

1. From the above examples it can be seen how the control of temperature of aggregates and cement is essential to control fresh concrete temperature.

2. In some countries such as those of the Arabian Peninsula, summer temperature can reach 45°C regularly and ice flakes are added to the concrete to cool it down to acceptable temperature on site.

Table 23 shows the example of Table 22 (A) with addition of 40 kg of ice and reduction of water to 110 kg to maintain the W/C ratio constant. This example shows how effective the addition of ice flakes is in lowering fresh concrete temperature in very hot climate.

Table 23. Example of Temperature at 70°C with Addition of 40 Kilograms of Ice and Reduction of Water to 100 Kilograms

Tc	70°C
Mc	380kg
Tfa	25°C
Mfa	800kg
Tca	35°C
Mca	1000kg
Tw	25°C
Mw	110kg
Mi	40kg
T	**26°C**

Admixtures Management

Admixtures in liquid form are dispensed directly in the concrete mixer. The dispensing system is designed to pump liquid admixtures from the storage tanks based on the mix design that has been input in the computer system.

Each liquid admixture is collected into specially designed transparent graduated cylinders where either a load cell or a volumetric valve controls the amount to be dosed per each cubic meter of concrete.

Because mix designs are proportioned by weight of components, admixtures are usually expressed in mass/m^3 even if some dispensing systems work based on dispensed volume, not dispensed weight.

The density of common admixtures may be found in the manufacturers' technical data sheet and it ranges from 1,050 kg/m^3 for polymeric admixtures to up to 1,180 kg/m^3 for naphthalene-based admixtures. Knowing the density allows conversion to mass into volume and vice versa.

Thus, if, for instance, 4.5 kg/m^3 of acrylic plasticizer (density 1'050 kg/m^3) are required in a mix design, the volume is given by the well-known relationship between mass, volume and density: *density=mass/volume* and it is given by: 0.0043 m^3, or 4.3 liters. The same mass of naphthalene-based admixture (density 1'180 kg/m^3) would yield 0.0038 m^{3}only, or 3.8 liters.

Admixtures are often also expressed in percentage of total cementitious materials. Again, percentage is expressed as mass of admixture divided by mass of cement. Hence, if a plasticizing admixture is dosed, for instance, at 3.5 kg with 380 kg of cement in the mix design, it can be expressed as 0.92%.

Usually, modern batching plants have two or three admixtures' dispensers. In projects where concrete must be delivered for long distances, in the summer and when freeze-thaw resistance of concrete is required, it is always recommended to have three lines available. One for superplasticizer, one for plasticizer-retarder, and one for the air-entraining admixture.

Systems that weigh admixtures are to be preferred to systems relying on volumetric measurement with butterfly valves. Sometimes these valves, if not well maintained, can block and allow undetected quantities of admixture to be pumped in the mixer, causing segregation if the admixture is a superplasticizer. If the admixture has retarding properties, this may cause issues with initial and final setting time of concrete.

Storage tanks for admixtures can be either 200-liter or 1,000-liter drums or larger tanks of up to 5,000 liters or 10,000 liters. Because admixtures are a suspension of solid particles in water, as seen previously in this chapter, they tend to settle when they are left unused in a container for a long time.

Thus, consumption of admixtures from 1,000-liter tanks must be relatively quick, or else a larger volume of storage is required, furnished with a circulation system to keep the admixture agitated.

Since the properties of admixtures are in fact all related to the properties of the solid fraction suspended in water, if settling takes place, the suspension becomes more concentrated at the bottom of the drum than at the top, causing pumping of more concentrated admixture first, followed, as production progresses, by a more diluted one.

This can cause dramatic changes in the initial workability and setting time of the concrete and it can negatively reflect on both fresh and hardened properties of the mix, as well as on the saw cut time of joints.

Finally, the environmental conditions must be kept into account when storing admixtures having a specific shelf life, and this shelf life can be shortened when exposed to excessive heat or excessive cold.

Thus, when ambient temperature is expected to consistently be on average 5°C or less, admixtures shall be stored indoor and they should never be left under the sun in the summer, but they should always be shaded in protected areas.

Precision of Weighing Equipment and Plant Calibration

Concrete mix designs are expressed in terms of mass of each component per 1 m³ of vibrated (or densified) concrete, i.e., concrete where all the natural air entrapped during production and placing is removed by means of vibration and consolidation. Vibration does not affect, generally, the volume of entrained air introduced with an air-entraining admixture.

Refer to batching plant report in Table 20. The first column is the mix design with dry components (aggregates in SSD condition). The second column is for the weight corrections for aggregates having a free moisture content (difference between moisture content and absorption) greater than zero.

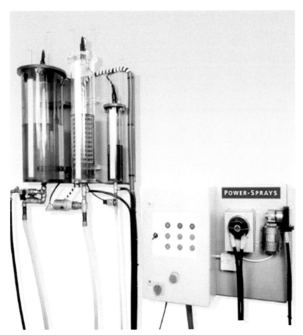

Transparent graduated cylinder A. The pipes at the bottom of the cylinders connect to the storage tanks, usually kept outdoors.

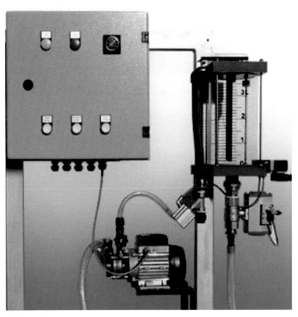

Transparent graduated cylinder B. Each liquid admixture is collected into specially designed transparent graduated cylinders.

1,000-Liter tank. Consumption of admixtures from 1,000-liter tanks must be relatively quick.

5,000-Liter Tank. This contains a flushing system to keep liquid in recirculation.

Table 24: Example of Concrete Mix Design or Batching Plant Report without Consideration of Water Absorption

	Mix Design	BATCHED		
Component	Mass (kg)	Mass (kg)	Moisture Content	Absorption
Cement	380	380		
Sand	750	776.3	5.00%	1.50%
5-10 mm	450	456.8	2.50%	1.00%
10-20 mm	745	748.7	1.50%	1.00%
Target water	152.0	115.3		
Water in aggregates	–	36.7		
Plasticizer	3.8	3.8		
Air entrainer	1.14	1.14		

SSD = saturated-surface-dry, mm = millimeter, kg = kilogram.

Refer to Table 18, where the unit weight and yield of concrete are 2,482 kg/m³ and 1.0 m³, respectively.

It will be expected that the automatic system of the plant would be able to match exactly the required weights of each component. However, as for any weighing device, there is only a certain amount of precision the instrument can provide, meaning that there is always a difference between target weight (the weight of components in the mix design) and the actual weight (what the system delivers in the mixer). This difference is the error of the measuring system.

In practice when the plant weighs, for example, 400 kg of cement (input or target value), the system will load the weighing scale of cement until it measures 400 kg, then cement will stop flowing on the scale. But the measured quantity will never match the input quantity, and the larger the discrepancy, the larger the error of the system is.

Table 25: Example of Concrete Mix Design or Batching Plant Report with Consideration of Water Absorption

Component	Mass (kg)	Density (kg/m³)	Volume (m³)
Cement	380	3100	0.1226
Sand (SSD)	750	2700	0.2778
5-10 mm (SSD)	450	2700	0.1667
10-20 mm (SSD)	745	2700	0.2759
Water	115.3	1000	0.1153
Free water in aggregates	36.7	1000	0.0367
Plasticizer	3.8	1180	0.0032
Air entrainer	1.14	1050	0.0011
Air content	–	–	0.04
Unit Weight	**2482**	**Volume**	**1.00**

SSD = saturated-surface-dry, mm = millimeter, kg = kilogram, m³ = cubic meter.

In particular "error" in percentage is the following ratio between the target and the measured (or actual) quantity: (actual-target)/target and we define as "tolerance" between the target and the measured quantity, the difference: (target-measured). Error is negative when the actual weight is smaller than target, and it is positive when the target weight is larger than target.

The larger the error of the weighing systems of the batching plant, the greater the deviation on the yield of concrete will be, as it will be shown in the following examples.

Table 23 shows an example of the calculated errors (%) between target weights of the mix design and actual weights dispensed in the mixer. It can be seen that each weighing system is dispensing with a certain error which, in this case, is always negative meaning that the actual weight dispensed by each weighing scale is always lower than target.

The result is that the yield of concrete is no longer 1.0 m³ but reduced to 0.97 m³. Due to this, the following important points must be highlighted in Table 23:

(i)   There are 15 kg less of cement per cubic meter in the mix design produced.
(ii)   There is a 3% deficiency in volume for each m³ produced.

Consider the example of an order of concrete to be delivered to form a concrete pavement having, for example, 300 m length, 10 m width, and 0.28 m thickness. The target vibrated volume is 840 m³.

However, if the plant produces systematically with the errors of Table 22, when 840 m³ of concrete will be delivered to site, 25.2m³ (or 3% of the target volume) will be missing and the formed pavement would be 9.0 m short in length.

The supplier in this case has had costs to produce 814.8 m³ only but has earned money as if 840m³ was produced. In addition, the contractor has paid the supplier to have 380 kg/m³ of cement to grant strength and durability and ends up receiving a concrete mix with less cement per cubic meter than required by the mix design. Finally, to complete the pavement, the contractor has to order (and pay) for additional 25.2 m³ of concrete.

Hence, the contractor is paying the supplier to receive less volume of concrete and of a lesser quality.

The outcome of this example is that the weight of concrete resulting from the combined errors of the weighing systems in the example above is 2,305 kg, which is not for a 1.0 m³ of concrete but for 0.97m³ only. The unit weight of concrete delivered is therefore 2,376 kg/m³ only (weight divided by actual yield).

Table 26: Example of Calculated Errors between Target Weights of the Mix Design and Actual Weights Dispensed in the Mixer
(%)

Component	Target Mass (kg)	Actual Mass (kg)	Error (%)	Density (kg/m³)	Target Volume (m³)	Actual Volume (m³)
Cement	380	365	-3.9%	3100	0.1226	0.1177
Sand (SSD)	750	697	-7.1%	2700	0.2778	0.2581
5-10 mm (SSD)	450	389	-13.6%	2700	0.1667	0.1441
10-20 mm (SSD)	745	702	-5.8%	2700	0.2759	0.2600
Water	115.3	110	-4.6%	1000	0.1153	0.1100
Free water in aggregates	36.7	36.7	0.0%	1000	0.0367	0.0367
Plasticizer	3.8	3.75	-1.3%	1180	0.0032	0.0032
Air entrainer	1.14	1.13	-0.9%	1050	0.0011	0.0011
Air content	--			--	0.04	0.04
Unit Weight	2482	2305		Volume	1.00	0.97

SSD = saturated-surface-dry, mm = millimeter, kg = kilogram, kg/m³ = kilogram per cubic meter.

The unit weight of concrete can be measured with the equipment and standards. The test is simple and takes few minutes to complete in the field. The test consists of vibrating a sample of concrete in a container of known volume (8.0 liters precisely) and by dividing the mass of concrete vibrated in the volume by the volume of the container.

By comparing the output of this test with the unit weight that is reported in the concrete mix design, it is possible to assess in the field whether the batching plant has some issues with precision of weighing scales.

Assume, for the case of Table 23, that the target unit weight as per mix design is 2,482 kg/m³ and that the unit weight test result is 2,342 kg/m³ and assume that the air content measured on the sample is 4% (40 liters or 0.04 m³) as targeted.

Because the measured unit weight is only 98.3% of the target unit weight, it is possible that the batching plant is weighing less of some components. We cannot know which component is underdosed, but this should prompt the receiver of the concrete to investigate further with the supplier on the possible causes of the discrepancy.

If, on the other side, the measured unit weight in the field is, for instance, 2,505 kg/m³ and we still assume that the air content measured on the sample is as per mix design (4%), it is 105% of the target unit weight, meaning that some components are now dosed in excess, usually aggregates. Having overdosed aggregates, especially sand, may cause issues with segregation and excess fines content on the surface, among others.

Usually, a tolerance on the yield of concrete larger than ± 1% and ± 2% of the target volume (1.0 m³) is not acceptable for non-air-entrained concrete and air-entrained concrete, respectively.

To ensure that errors of the weighing system are limited, British Standards Institution 2021 requires the weighing scales of each component in the batching plant to be precise as shown in Table 24.

Consider, for example, a cement weighing scale that is calibrated by an independent metrology body. The scale works within the range 0–2,000 kg. Thus, 20% of full-scale is 200 kg. Hence, from the definition of error as (actual – target)/target, there can only be a maximum error of ±4.0 kg between target and actual weight up to 200 kg of cement dosed, and from 200 kg to 1,000 kg of cement dosed the maximum error can be ±10 kg.

The same considerations are valid also for precision by volume as for the case, as seen previously, of some dispensing equipment for liquid admixtures.

The determination of the precision of a batching plant's weighing and/or volumetric system must be carried out at any new installation or commissioning and, periodically, once a year. If field yield tests provide strong indications that there might be issues with precision of the system because of unit weight of concrete in defect or in excess of the mix design value, new calibrations should be made.

Table 27: Weight of Each Component in a Batching Plant

	Load/Volume Interval	
Where batching by mass	0%–20% of full-scale load	20%–100% of full-scale load
Maximum error in % of the load	± 2%	± 1%
Where batching by volume	< 30 l	> 30 l
Maximum error in % of the volume	± 3%	± 2%

Calibrations must be carried out by certified bodies operating in the country under the recognition and/or accreditation of public authorities.

EN 206-1:2013 provides tolerances for the batching process of each constituent material. Table 25 reports the tolerances.

These should not be confused with errors of weighing scales. While errors provide the precision of the weighing systems, tolerances are defined as those changes to the concrete mix that are tolerated before defining the mix a different mix design. This is called fine-tuning and is defined as all of the minor changes that can be applied to the proportions of components without changing the properties of the mix design.

Table 28 presents the tolerances for fine-tuning for the mix design of Table 23. These tolerances allow the producer to adjust the mix design without changing its basic properties.

Table 29 shows the tolerances calculated for the mix design based on sample calculations presented in Table 23.

Table 28: Tolerances for Fine-Tuning for Mix Design

Constituent Material	Tolerance
Cement/Cementitious materials Water Total Aggregates	± 3% of required quantity
Admixtures	± 5% of required quantity

Note: Values are based on the sample calculations in Table 23.

Table 29: Tolerances Calculated for the Mix Design

		Tolerance	
Cement	380 kg	±11.4 kg	
Sand (SSD)	750 kg	±22.5 kg	
5-10 mm (SSD)	450 kg	±13.5 kg	±3%
10-20 mm (SSD)	745 kg	±22.4 kg	
Water	115.3 kg	±3.50 kg	
Plasticizer	3.8 kg	±0.20 kg	±5%
Air entrainer	1.14 kg	±0.060 kg	

SSD = saturated-surface-dry, mm = millimeter, kg = kilogram.

Note: values are based on the sample calculations in Table 23.

4

Management of Stress Relief Joints

A. Introduction and Overview

Jointed plain concrete pavements (JPCPs) for roads and highways rely on joints to control deformations and to relieve stresses and deflections induced by:

(i) contraction and/or expansion in the longitudinal direction, and
(ii) warping/curling in the transversal direction.

This chapter outlines the main material-related factors of influence for the performance of stress relief joints only, precisely—transversal contraction joints, and expansion joints.

Longitudinal contraction joints work in similar fashion to transversal contraction joints, while longitudinal construction joints are not influenced much by material-related factors and will not be considered here.

Uncontrolled contraction or expansion in the longitudinal direction causes tensile stresses and compressive stresses to build up, which may cause cracking to appear in JPCPs. As seen in Chapter 1, concrete pavements contract as a result of drying shrinkage and thermal shrinkage.

Drying shrinkage is the decrease in volume caused by evaporation of some of the water in excess to the amount required to fully hydrate cement grains (approximately, only some 25% of the mass of cement in the concrete mix will be consumed for the hydration process). Since more than 25% of water by mass of cement is used to produce concrete for pavements, there is always a certain amount of evaporable water causing drying shrinkage to take place in the concrete in the first days, weeks, and months after placing.

Thermal shrinkage is the contraction caused by a change in temperature of the pavement from a higher value to a lower value. Thermal shrinkage occurs either when newly cast concrete heats up in the first days because of the exothermal reactions between water and cement and then it cools down to ambient temperature, or when the season changes from summer to winter. Thermal shrinkage is controlled by the coefficient of thermal expansion (and contraction) of concrete.

Because concrete is not free to contract in the longitudinal direction due to the restraint provided by the support (granular material or cement stabilized base), drying and thermal shrinkage will induce transverse crack periodically spaced, as presented in Chapter 1.

On the other hand, when the temperature of concrete is raised in service due to exposure to increased ambient temperature, the pavement will expand causing compressive stresses to build-up within the pavement (Figure 8, for example) and in adjoined structures (bridges' abutments for instance). The magnitude of expansion or contraction is, once again, directly related to the coefficient of thermal expansion of concrete.

Also, as discussed in Chapter 1, under hot–cold and wet–dry cycles, concrete pavements warp and curl in the transversal direction causing them to locally detach from the foundation in the corners, in the edges or in the center, depending on the nature and magnitude of thermal gradients, thus creating points of weakness under traffic loads.

To prevent this, longitudinal contraction joints are formed in concrete pavements to control the locations of cracks that might otherwise form randomly due to restrained temperature- and moisture-related movements (i.e., shrinkage, thermal contraction, curling, and warping). When possible, longitudinal contraction joints are generally cut at locations that coincide with pavement lane lines to facilitate lane delineation and traffic control.

Longitudinal construction joints are the result of adjacent placements of concrete pavement. As discussed in Chapter 1, tie bars are used as load transfer mechanism for longitudinal joints.

B. Transversal Contraction Joints

To control where cracking induced by contraction movements will appear, equally spaced saw-cut transversal contraction joints are built in JPCPs. These joints control contraction due to shrinkage, and when they are properly built and functional, they also control expansion caused by the seasonal increase of pavement temperature in passing from winter to summer.

As discussed in Chapter 1, joints work on the principle of creating a plane of weakness where the saw cut is made. This induces cracks to be localized at these points of weakness and, thus, to be controlled. Contraction joints can be dummy or dowelled.

Dummy contraction joints rely solely on aggregate interlock to grant sufficient load transfer efficiency across the joint. Load transfer efficiency (LTE) is defined as the ratio between the deflection of the approach slab versus the deflection of the leave slab.

An LTE of 100% means that, when load moves from the approach slab to the leave slab, the deflection is the same on both sides of the joint, meaning that load is fully transmitted. An LTE of 0% means that only the entry slab is deflected while the leave slab remains undeflected, meaning that load is not transmitted at all. Usually, LTE from 25% to 60% is observed in functional pavements in service.

Because aggregate interlock depends, keeping all other factors constant (aggregates size, shape, roundness, volume fraction in the concrete mix, etc.), on the crack opening, and because from about 1.5 mm of crack opening, interlock is virtually lost as seen in Chapter 1, dummy joints are generally used only in low-trafficked roads, i.e., roads that, according to Reference 27, receive less than 100 passes per day from trucks.

Dowelled joints, on the other side, rely on the load transfer provided by steel dowels to ensure that the joint has always a minimum LTE regardless how wide the joint is in maximum contraction.

The purpose of dowels is to transfer load across a joint without impeding joint opening and closing in response to daily and seasonal changes in temperature causing slabs to contract and to expand. This means that one end of each dowel must be greased or cased to allow free longitudinal movement on one end of the joint.

Studies indicate that the use of dowels is beneficial for all conventional jointed concrete pavements in providing load transfer and maintaining the horizontal and vertical alignment of the slabs. The use of dowel bars at contraction joints is recommended for all roadways.

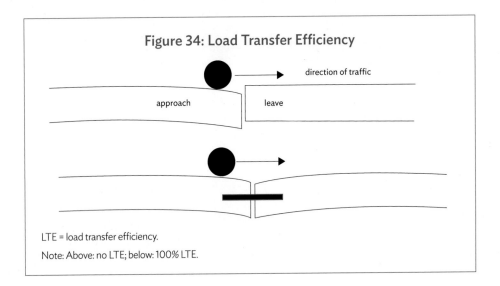

Figure 34: Load Transfer Efficiency

LTE = load transfer efficiency.

Note: Above: no LTE; below: 100% LTE.

Important Factors for the Design of Transversal Contraction Joints

The most critical factor to be considered when designing transversal contraction joints in concrete pavement is related to the expected joint opening. Other factors are traffic volumes, dictating whether dummy or dowelled/tied joints are required, or traffic patterns.

Joint opening can be expressed by eq-1 of Chapter 1 reported below for reference once again:

$$\Delta L = C \cdot L(\alpha \Delta T + \varepsilon)$$

Where:

(i) ΔL – joint opening (mm)
(ii) C – restraint coefficient from support (taken as 0.65 for cement treated base, 0.80 for granular base)
(iii) L – distance between two consecutive joints (i.e. panel's or slab's length) (mm)
(iv) α – coefficient of thermal expansion of concrete (CTE) ($\mu\varepsilon$/°C)
(v) ΔT – difference in pavement temperature between the temperature when the joint was formed and the minimum temperature the pavement will be subjected to in service (°C)
(vi) ε – hydraulic shrinkage of concrete (assumed, as we have seen in Chapter 1, to be 400 $\mu\varepsilon$)

Note:
$1.0 = \mu\varepsilon = 1.0/1,000,000 = 1.0 \cdot 10^{-6} = 0.0001\%$

Thus, the prediction of joints opening is mainly a function of material properties such as the coefficient of thermal expansion (CTE) and drying shrinkage, which need therefore to be predicted accurately.

Let us assume that a joint is formed in autumn with ambient temperature of 10°C and that the minimum temperature the pavement will be exposed to is –10°C, thus to a thermal differential of 20°C. Taking a CTE of 10.0 $\mu\varepsilon$/°C and a shrinkage of 400 $\mu\varepsilon$, as seen in Chapter 1, we calculate, for a slab's length of 5,000 mm resting on cement treated base, a joint opening ΔL = 1.95 mm.

With the same assumptions above, except that we take a joint formed at an ambient temperature of 30°C (summer, thus with a thermal differential of 40°C this time), we calculate a joint opening in the winter equal to ΔL = 2.60 mm.

The implications of this can be found in the choice of the joint sealant. Sealants are used to protect the joint from blockage by particles and debris flushed by the rain on the pavement. These particles, which penetrate when the joint is in maximum expansion (as discussed in Chapter 1), prevent the joint to contract back when temperature is increased (from winter to summer) and may cause blowups at the joint (Chapters 1 and 6). To prevent particles and water to penetrate the joint, sealants are used. Sealants can be pre-formed or poured (hot-poured or cold-poured) (Table 26).

Pre-formed sealants are placed in a reservoir, which needs to accommodate the sealant and to which the sealant must adhere even when the concrete is in maximum contraction (maximum opening of the joint). This means that the sealant must be compressed in the reservoir at all times and it must expand progressively as the joint opens while retaining some amount of compression. Thus, the sealant cannot be allowed to expand back to its nominal width.

If, on the other side, the joint opens to the point that compression in the sealant is lost, the sealant will detach from the joint wall, it will become lose and it will deteriorate faster, allowing particles to block progressively the joint.

Pre-formed sealants can be described with the following parameters:

(i)   Nominal width W_{seal}, which is the width of the sealant at rest.
(ii)   Maximum movement ΔW_{seal} in percentage, which is the maximum amount of compression/expansion that the sealant can sustain (sometimes this parameter is expressed as percentage of the nominal width).
(iii) If ΔL is the joint opening, a reservoir of width $W_{reservoir}$ will experience an increase of width (in %) of: $\Delta L/W_{reservoir}$. The sealant inserted in the reservoir must also have the same increase in width ΔW_{seal}. Thus, we can write the following identity:

$$\Delta W_{seal} = \Delta L/W_{reservoir}$$

From which we can express the width of reservoir as:

$$W_{reservoir} = \Delta L/\Delta W_{seal}$$

For a predicted joint opening ΔL of 2.60 mm and a typical value of ΔW_{seal} for pre-formed sealants of 50%, we calculate $W_{reservoir}$ = 5.2 mm. This is the minimum value of the reservoir's design width. This should be compared to the standard width of commercially pre-formed sealants usually ranging from 11 mm to 76 mm. An 11 mm pre-formed seal with 50% compressibility and extensibility can be compressed only to max 5.5 mm for instance, and it will remain in compression when the reservoir opens to 7.8 mm (5.2 mm + 2.6 mm). Hence, for this example, the width of the reservoir must be increased to 6.0 mm and a 11.0 mm wide pre-formed seal with 50% extensibility may be used.

Poured sealants are placed in the reservoir of width $W_{reservoir}$ and they must elongate following to the reservoir's opening. In this case, the width of the reservoir is predefined and the choice of the type of sealant follows from the value of elongation at break reported in the manufacturer's data sheet, which is the amount of extension it can sustain before breaking at a certain temperature. Because poured sealants are polymeric in nature and because polymers become stiff and brittle at low temperature, the elongation at break is generally assessed, for safety, at below freezing temperature in the laboratory.

Assume again that the calculated joint opening ΔL is 3.0 mm for a reservoir of width 10.0 mm. It is expected the sealant to extend not less than 30% to allow its width to increase from $W_{reservoir}$ to $W_{reservoir} + \Delta L$. Choosing a hot-poured sealant with an elongation at break of, for example, 50% would ensure the sealant to expand without breaking. If the expected joint opening is larger, say 8.0 mm, and the width of reservoir is kept at 10.0 mm, the sealant chosen must now have at least 80% elongation. If such sealant is not available in the market, the width of the reservoir must be increased for instance to 15.0 mm so that the minimum elongation required for the sealant is 53% only, and so on.

Pre-formed sealants. A reservoir is used to compress sealants to allow them to expand progressively, as the joint opens while retaining some amount of compression.

Poured sealants. Also placed in a reservoir, poured sealants must elongate following the reservoir's opening.

A list of poured and pre-formed sealants is given in Table 30 along with reference to ASTM / AASHTO standard specifications.

Table 30: Poured and Pre-Formed Sealants

Material Category	Material Type	Specification(s)	Description
Liquid, Hot- Applied Sealants	Polymerized/	ASTM 0 6690, Type I (AASHTO M324)	Moderate climates, 50% extension at 0°F (18°C)
	Rubberized Asphalts		
Liquid, Hot- Applied Sealants	Polymerized/	ASTM 0 6690, Type II (AASHTO M324)	Most climates, 50% extension at -20°F
	Rubberized Asphalts		(-29°C)
Liquid, Hot- Applied Sealants	Polymerized/	ASTM 0 6690, Type III (AASHTO M324)	Most climates, 50% extension at -20°F
	Rubberized Asphalts		(-29°C) with other special tests
Liquid, Hot- Applied Sealants	Polymerized/	ASTM 0 6690, Type IV	Very cold climates, 200% extension at
	Rubberized Asphalts	(AASHTO M 324)	-20°F (-29°C)
Liquid, Cold/ Ambient- Applied Sealants	Single-Component Silicone	ASTM 0 5893, Type NS	Non-sag, toolable, low modulus
Liquid, Cold/Ambient- Applied Sealants	Single-Component Silicone	ASTM 0 5893, Type SL	Self-leveling, no tooling, low modulus
Liquid, Cold/ Ambient- Applied Sealants	Two-Component Elastomeric Polymer (polysulfides, polyurethanes)	Fed Spec SS·S·200E, Type M	Jet-fuel resistant,
			Jet-blast resistant,
			Machine-applied fast cure
Liquid, Cold/ Ambient- Applied Sealants	Elastomeric Polymer (polysulfides, polyurethanes)	Fed Spec SS·S·200E, Type H	Jet-fuel resistant,
			Jet-blast resistant,
			Hand-mixed retarded cure
Solid, Cold/ Ambient- Applied Sealants	Preformed Compression Seals	ASTM 0 2628	Jet-fuel resistant preformed seal
	– Polychloroprene Elastomeric (Neoprene)	ASTM 0 2835	Used in installation of preformed seal
	– Lubricant		
Expansion Joint Filler	Preformed Filler Material	ASTM 0 1751 (AASHTO M 213)	Bituminous, non- extruding, resilient
Expansion Joint Filler	Preformed Filler Material	ASTM 0 1752, Types HV (AASHTO M 153)	Sponge rubber, cork, and recycled PVC
Expansion Joint Filler	Preformed Filler Material	ASTM 0 994 (AASHTO M33)	Bituminous
Backer Rod (if used)	-	ASTM 0 5249	For hot- or cold-applied sealants

Other geometrical parameters of importance for the performance of sealants besides width are depth (D) and recess depth (r) (Figures 35 and 36).

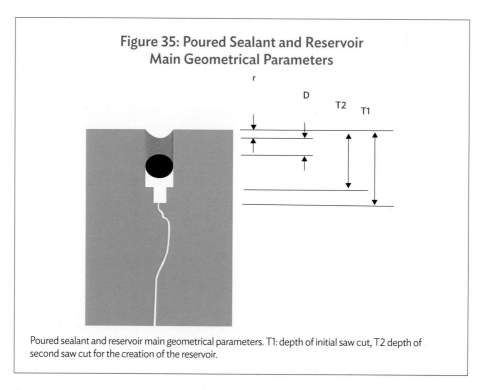

Figure 35: Poured Sealant and Reservoir Main Geometrical Parameters

Poured sealant and reservoir main geometrical parameters. T1: depth of initial saw cut, T2 depth of second saw cut for the creation of the reservoir.

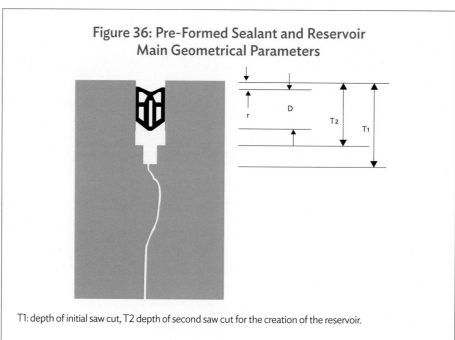

Figure 36: Pre-Formed Sealant and Reservoir Main Geometrical Parameters

T1: depth of initial saw cut, T2 depth of second saw cut for the creation of the reservoir.

C. Expansion Joints

A special-use transversal joint is the expansion joint. It is constructed in new pavements to relieve potential excessive slab expansion or movement without developing compressive stresses in the pavement that might result in joint spalling and blowups in the pavement or damage to adjacent structures (e.g., bridge decks and approach panels).

Expansion joints typically include dowels or other load transfer devices and allow independent movement only in the direction of expansion through and expansion cap (Figure 37).

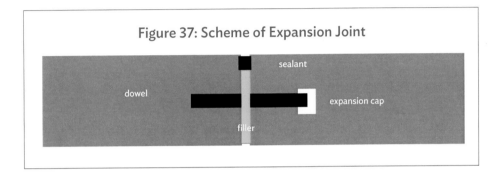

Figure 37: Scheme of Expansion Joint

Expansion joints are always required for transitioning between the JPCP and other adjacent structures, such as bridge abutments, for instance, or existing pavements. Without functional expansion joints, pavements may exert very high stresses on existing structures when they expand from winter to summer, which may also lead to cracking and large-scale blowups in the pavement.

On the other side, the frequent use of expansion joints to relieve compressive stresses within JPCP should be carefully evaluated for the following reasons. If dowelled contraction joints are built with aligned dowels greased on one end, the seasonal and day/night movements of adjacent slabs are not restrained. In this case using periodically spaced expansion joints at, for example, 80–100 m, may not be entirely justified.

Assuming a 100 m long stretch of JPCP is separated by two expansion joints at the ends and contraction joints have spacing of 5.0 m—this means that a 100 m long stretch of pavement contains two expansion joints and 18 contraction joints. Also assuming the joints were formed in the summer and they will therefore experience—as has been seen in previous sections—considerable opening in the winter. If the anticipated contraction or expansion is, for instance 3.0 mm at each joint and all joints are functional, this translates to 54 mm of free expansion.

Designing expansion joints periodically spaced within the JPCP means to assume that contraction joints are not fully functional and expansion is restrained. However, if contraction joints, especially close to the location of the expansion joint, are in fact functional, the presence of a nearby expansion joint causes contraction joints in proximity to the expansion joint to open more, while other joints at a distance from the expansion joint may not open at all. This may cause unbalanced stresses development and localized blowups as well as the blocking of open contraction joints by incompressible material. The implications of overusing expansion joints for nearby contraction joints. On the other hand, if 100% of contraction joints are functional, there is no stress build-up at the ends of a 100 m stretch of pavement.

Using Hooke's law to relate strain and stress through the modulus of elasticity of concrete (assumed to be 27,600 MPa as shown in Table 2), and neglecting the effects of creep, we have a total compressive stress in longitudinal direction associated with totally nonfunctional joints within a 100 m (100,000 mm) long stretch expanding from winter to summer of:

$$\alpha = E \cdot \varepsilon = 27600 \cdot 5.4 \cdot 10^{-5} = 15.0 \ MPa$$

Where:

$$\varepsilon = 54 \ mm/100{,}000 \ mm = 5.4 \cdot 10^{-5}$$

Hence, on each end of the stretch, 7.50 MPa compressive stress may build.

If the stretch is 200 m long, the stress on each end would be 15.0 MPa, sufficient to cause blowups within the pavement and to exert high shear / tensile stresses in nearby structures.

Hence, the most important thing is to have as many functional contraction joints in service as possible. This means building joints with aligned, equally spaced dowels greased on one end and to provide proper periodic maintenance to avoid the joints to become blocked by incompressible materials.

The joints opening must be predicted accurately to enhance the service life of the joint and of the sealant, as seen previously. Then, periodic expansion joints may be inserted as a safety measure to relieve compressive stresses within the pavement in case some joints become nonfunctional during the service life of the pavement.

The expansion joints should be used in the following cases:

(i)   the pavement is divided into long panels (18–20 m or more) without contraction joints,
(ii)   the pavement is constructed while ambient temperatures are below 4°C,
(iii) contraction joints are allowed to be infiltrated by large incompressible materials, and
(iv)   the pavement is constructed with aggregates that have high expansion characteristics.

If a pavement is built in the winter (item 2) it will expand in the next summer by an amount proportional to the difference in temperature between winter and summer. Thus, while pavements built in winter will have little contraction and larger expansion in the summer, pavements built in the summer will have little expansion leading to higher contraction in the winter. Thus, mostly pavements built in cold environment will experience higher compressive stresses when temperature increases.

Also, if the expected level of workmanship is poor (meaning that items 3 and item 4 are likely events), expansion joints may still be needed to relieve stresses induced by poorly functional contraction joints. In any case, expansion joints are mandatory to relieve potential compressive stresses forming at the interface between the pavement and existing structures.

D. Formation of Expansion Joints

Special care must be given to constructing functional expansion joints. Unlike transversal contraction joints, which are formed by saw cutting the pavement, expansion joints require the formation of two transversal construction joints.

Thus, a paving machine may not be used to pave the final part of a pavement ending with an expansion joint. In this case, the last portion of the paved width must be cast manually. The concrete mix for this operation may be the same mix design used for machine paving, with a higher slump but usually not exceeding 100 mm.

Figure 38 presents a plan view sketch (top) where black dotted lines are dowelled transverse contraction joints, the red dotted line is a dowelled transversal formed construction joint and the last panel (in blue color) between the construction joint and the expansion joint (black strip) is cast manually likewise the first panel immediately after the expansion joint (if applicable). The transversal construction joint may be formed by saw cutting for the entire width and depth the end of the machine-paved stretch and by manually drilling dowels on the vertical face of the newly formed construction joint to link to the adjacent panel which is cast manually (Figure 38).

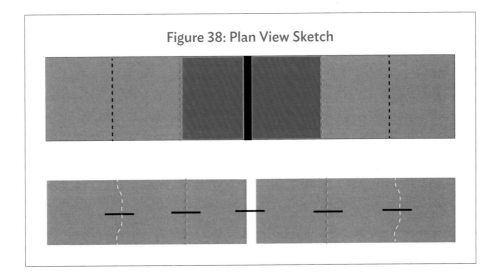

Figure 38: Plan View Sketch

An alternative to dowelled expansion joints is thickened edge slabs. When thickening is equal to 1.25T, where T is design thickness of the concrete pavement, although LTE is zero according to what has been stated in this handbook, deflections are now reduced not by dowels but by an increased edged thickness. Hence, dowel-less expansion joint may be constructed providing the two opposite slabs forming the joint have thickened edges in correspondence of the joint. Recommendations on the formation of thickened edge slabs are given in the references of this handbook.

5

Curing of Concrete Pavements

A. Introduction and Overview

Curing may be defined as the action taken to maintain moist conditions on the surface of a freshly placed cementitious mixture to allow hydration to progress, so that the potential properties of the mixture may develop, and early cracking phenomena are minimized.

As seen in previous chapters, curing is essential for JPCPs because it reduces the rate of evaporation of water from the pavement surface, it increases durability and, keeping all other factors constant, it also improves the freeze-thaw resistance. Also, because JPCPs are non-reinforced, they are more prone to cracking than reinforced concrete, which makes the curing even more important for preventing excessive restrained contraction.

Because pavements have a large surface area, they tend to lose surface moisture at very high rate, and this is exacerbated by unfavorable weather conditions (wind, low humidity, high temperature). Short-term (within few hours) loss of water from a horizontal concrete surface causes plastic shrinkage, while long-term (weeks, months) loss of water from a horizontal surface causes drying shrinkage. Both phenomena relate to some form of restrained contraction and as such—as extensively discussed in Chapters 1 and 4—they may lead to uncontrolled cracking.

Plastic shrinkage is a very common phenomenon appearing on concrete surfaces cast in unfavorable conditions such as high wind and low humidity. Any time concrete is placed and vibrated, there will be some amount of water bleeding, which consists, in the appearance on the surface of fresh concrete, of a film of water (causing the surface of concrete to have a sheen). This film is beneficial because it acts as a natural curing agent for the concrete surface. In low-humidity conditions, however, this bleed water rapidly evaporates and the rate of evaporation on the surface is much higher than the rate of evaporation deeper in the concrete section.

Hence, the top 50–100 mm of concrete contract at a faster rate than the rest of the volume, and the result of this internally restrained contraction are surface cracks forming within few hours from placing. At this time, the tensile strength of concrete is negligible, and these cracks easily break the paste but propagate only a few centimeters downward, usually losing all their energy when they encounter a coarse aggregate particle.

Plastic shrinkage cracks can be all oriented in the same direction when prevailing wind is the main cause, in which case the direction of cracks is generally perpendicular to the direction of prevailing wind. Or they can be randomly oriented as shown in Figure 39, when wind is gusting from different directions and/or when the rate of evaporation is caused by the very high ambient temperature (in excess of 35°C) and exposure to direct sunlight.

Plastic shrinkage cracks can be wide on the surface (1–2 mm wide or more), but they rapidly disappear with depth, usually within the top 80–100 mm. The general rule for this type of cracks is that when they do not exceed more than 33% of the slab's thickness, they are not considered as major defects and they can be sealed. When these cracks, however, are frequent over a limited surface area, it may become uneconomical to repair them and replacing the affected concrete slabs may be advisable.

In continental/hot climate, the most critical time of the year for the appearance of plastic shrinkage cracks is in the summer. Any time air temperature is above 30°C, concrete temperature is at about 28°C–30°C or more, relative humidity is less than 50% and wind speed exceeds 3 km/h, the rate of evaporation of concrete with a W/C ratio equal or less than 0.45 and a dosage of cement exceeding 350 kg/m³ becomes critical for the onset of early cracking phenomena.

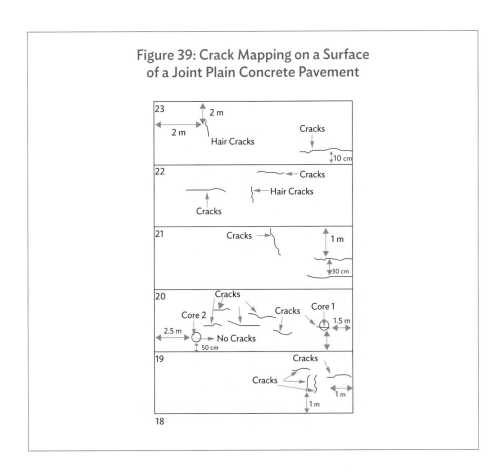

Figure 39: Crack Mapping on a Surface of a Joint Plain Concrete Pavement

This guide recommends the following precautions to minimize plastic shrinkage cracking:

(i)   have sufficient personnel, equipment, and supplies on hand to place and finish the concrete promptly;
(ii)   prevent concrete from drying too quickly between finishing operations;
(iii) start curing the concrete as soon as possible;
(iv)   in very hot, dry weather, use evaporation retarders;
(v)   consider placing the concrete in late afternoon; early evening, or at night; and
(vi)   make the concrete set faster.

Plastic shrinkage crack. Core extracted from the top surface shows a wide crack on the surface but rapidly ending at about 70 mm depth in a coarse aggregate.

Making the concrete set faster is particularly important when using some of the retarding admixtures described in Chapter 3. All cracks showed in the photo have formed, for instance, because the concrete mix design delayed setting from the moment it was placed (in the night) to the next morning hours when it was exposed to direct sunlight, when still partly fresh, in a very hot environment (>40°C air temperature) at tropical latitude. In this case, the mix design had to be reviewed and the retarder initially added separately to the mix was eliminated.

Drying shrinkage is the medium- and long-term volume contraction caused by progressive loss of evaporable water present in the capillary voids of concrete that are not involved in cement hydration, as seen in Chapter 3. Here, unlike plastic shrinkage, where restraint is internal and caused by differential contraction within the concrete thickness, contraction happens throughout the entire thickness of concrete and it is externally restrained by the foundation. High friction in the foundation (granular base or cement treated base) causes more restraint and increases the risk of shrinkage cracks in the concrete pavement.

Drying shrinkage cracks. Drying shrinkage cracks formed because the transversal contraction joints were cut too late and did not exactly control location of contraction. This type of crack starts at the bottom and moves upward.

Shrinkage cracks form when already tensile strength and elasticity modulus of concrete are high. Concrete is brittle and the cracks, once they form, have enough elastic energy to propagate for the entire thickness of the concrete.

Unlike plastic shrinkage cracks, drying shrinkage cracks cause concrete to decrease its mechanical properties, because full depth cracked concrete has lower flexural strength than undisturbed concrete. Hence, when uncontrolled drying shrinkage cracks form, they are a major defect, and all the affected concrete slabs should be removed and replaced. For JPCPs these cracks are allowed to form only, as seen in previous chapters, at saw cut transversal contraction joints.

B. Types of Curing

To control plastic and drying shrinkage cracking, the surface of the concrete must either lose as little internal moisture as possible, or else it needs to be kept moist with the addition of external moisture. When the surface of concrete is prevented from losing water without adding external moisture, the process is called **chemical curing**. While, when moisture is added, the process is called **wet or moist curing**. Combinations of wet curing and chemical curing are also common in concrete pavements.

Chemical Curing

Chemical curing includes **evaporation retarders and curing compounds**. Chemical curing is a type of curing that is used as soon as practically possible to reduce the rate of surface evaporation and to reduce the risk of cracking of JPCPs. Due to the peculiar features of concrete pavements (large surface area, lack of reinforcement) this is an essential step when casting JPCPs especially in desert-like, arid conditions experienced in some geographical locations.

Evaporation retarders are polyvinyl-alcohol-based compounds that are used to form an oil-like film on the surface of the concrete. Application rates are typically about 5.0 m^2/l. The guidance of the manufacturer should be followed with respect to application techniques and amounts.

For JPCPs, they typically are sprayed on the surface immediately after initial leveling of concrete is completed but before the texturing of the surface begins. However, these products dry very quickly thus requiring either multiple applications until concrete hardens or to be followed, after texturing of concrete is completed, by curing compounds. At this stage, before the curing compound is applied, fogging is also a suitable way to keep the surface of concrete moist.

The term **curing compound** is the generic definition applied to the family of products known as **liquid membrane-forming compounds**. These are by far the most common types of chemical compounds used to cure concrete pavements and they are frequently used to replace moist curing at once. These products are sprayed on a concrete surface as a liquid, that subsequently forms a membrane and so it reduces evaporation from that surface.

The aim is to maintain the relative humidity of the concrete surface above 80% for a few days (preferably up to a minimum of 3 days). Curing compounds provide the best available approach to balancing the needs of curing large surfaces of concrete with minimum negative impacts. Concrete cured with membrane-forming curing compounds has been shown to have better resistance to deicing salts than one cured with an external supply of water.

These compounds are typically based on waxes, and resins emulsified in water or solvent. In comparative testing, a compound based on chlorinated rubber was found to be the most effective, followed by the solvent-based compounds, and the least effective was the water-based type. Newer products based on poly alpha-methylstyrene are proving to be particularly effective.

There are two main types of curing compounds based on color. Type 1 materials are clear and primarily used for architectural applications, especially surfaces that are not intended to receive any other covering. Type 2 materials are white pigmented to increase reflectivity and are generally used in desert-like climate.

There are two classes of curing compounds, referring to the active ingredient. Class A is unrestricted with the active ingredients often being wax or linseed-oil-based materials. The active ingredients of Class B materials are required to be resins.

Curing compounds should be applied using spray equipment immediately after final finishing of the concrete (this includes texturing for JPCPs). The concrete surface should be damp, but bleeding should be effectively complete, and the sheen should have evaporated before the product is applied.

Complete coverage of the whole surface is essential. Sufficient material must be applied to account for the tendency of the material to run down into the texture or local low spots. If two coats are necessary to ensure complete coverage, then the second coat should be applied at right angles to the first.

White-pigmented curing compound. Nonhomogenous application of white-pigmented curing compound on a strip of an airfield's concrete pavement.

Water- and Moisture- Related Curing (Wet Curing)

Wet curing consists of applying water on the surface of the concrete when its internal moisture is rapidly lost due to desiccation. Water on the surface of concrete may only be applied after final setting, to avoid surface washout of fresh concrete paste. Among the many techniques available for wet curing of concrete, only the wet burlap is generally used in some cases where concrete is highly prone to shrinkage cracking even when curing compounds are used.

Fogging, which is the spraying of nebulized water droplets through nozzles, is also an effective and very early means to keep the surface of concrete moist between placing and applying the final curing compound. Here, because water is in the form of microscopic droplets, the application can be made also on fresh concrete without risking any surface washout.

Wet burlaps are sheets of natural or synthetic fabric that are kept moist for some time after concrete is set. Frequently, once the burlap is initially saturated with water, it is firmly covered by plastic to prevent evaporation and to provide a sort of "greenhouse effect" to the surface. The risk with this method is that if burlap and sheets are not firmly anchored to the pavement they can easily be blown away by strong wind.

The advantage of wet curing is that it is, by far, the most effective way of curing concrete in general to maximize durability and minimize cracking. The disadvantage is that from a logistical standpoint, it may be problematic in areas where access to usable water (i.e., water that is not contaminated by aggressive species for concrete such as chloride and sulfates, among the main ones) is limited. Thus, chemical curing using adequate products, which can eliminate the need of wet curing is generally preferred for concrete-paving operations.

Panels protected with soaked burlap. A strip of concrete protected first with burlap and covered with a plastic sheet is also visible in the background.

C. The Planning of Curing

Curing must be planned based on the type of concrete mix design and on the desired long-term properties. Low slump, low W/C ratio, high cement concrete mixes for pavements, are at a very high risk of early cracking in summer conditions and/or when relative humidity is low. The rate of bleeding for this type of concrete is generally low and therefore there is a deficit in surface moisture all the time during initial hours which are the most critical for plastic shrinkage cracking.

Concrete for pavements should therefore always be cured chemically by utilizing a suitable, highly reflective, high moisture retention curing compound to be applied after finishing the surface and after all bleed water (if any) is stopped.

However, there are cases where concrete may be prone to cracking as soon as it has been placed, due to adverse weather conditions (strong wind). These extreme conditions should generally lead to the cancellation of any placing of concrete. Yet, if concrete placing is done despite adverse weather conditions, the time between placing and finishing and texturing might be too wide for the concrete surface to resist cracking. In these cases, evaporation retarders are highly recommended at first, followed by curing compounds.

Regardless of the curing strategy adopted, the minimum efficiency of the curing system for pavements should be to keep surface of concrete at above 80% relative humidity for no less than 3 days. Beyond 3 days, concrete properties are generally sufficiently developed to resist shrinkage cracking, which is additionally controlled after the first few hours from placing when transversal contraction joints are formed.

6

Common Defects in Concrete Pavements

This chapter presents some non-exhaustive examples of common defects that may be observed in concrete pavements in service. The main features of each defect and the likely causes for its occurrence are described in the next pages by means of synthetic data sheets.

It should be noted that such defects may appear at any time after the concrete pavement has entered into service. However, the sooner these defects appear (within the first few years of service), the greater the chances of being caused by poor design, poor construction, poor maintenance, deficient specifications, and/or deficient quality of materials used.

Concrete pavements are usually designed with a target service life of not less than 20–30 years. This means that, under periodic ordinary maintenance, it will reasonably take at least 20–30 years for more than 10% of the surface of the concrete to show distresses that may impair riding quality, safety, and resistance to stresses from traffic and the environment.

Figure 40: Common Defects in Concrete Pavements

NAME	NATURE	FEATURES
Blocked Joint	Related to quality of materials, inadequate design, poor maintenance, poor construction practice	Incompressible material (sand, debris) is transported within the joint when concrete is in seasonal contraction, impeding therefore the next seasonal expansion

CAUSES	CONSEQUENCES
• Underestimation of coefficient of thermal expansion • Poor maintenance of the joint • Poor quality of sealant • Inadequate sealant	• Build-up of internal compressive stresses that may cause blowups at the joint

NAME	NATURE	FEATURES
Corner Crack	Related to poor design, poor construction	Due to warping or curling stresses, the corner of a concrete slab detaches from the ground losing support

CAUSES	CONSEQUENCES
• Lack of load transfer through tie bars across longitudinal joints	• Traffic passes over the unsupported slab may cause flexural cracking • Cracking causes water to permeate in the ground, which may reduce the bearing capacity

NAME	NATURE	FEATURES
D-cracks	Related to quality of aggregates, inadequate specifications	Due to the presence of coarse aggregates (diameter >20 mm) with poor freeze-thaw resistance, concrete paste is stressed by frost induced expansion of these aggregates and it cracks near areas of low restraint (i.e., near joints)

CAUSES	CONSEQUENCES
• Use of coarse aggregates with poor freeze-thaw resistance (aggregates with high porosity and weak particles)	• Cracks may merge and cause diffuse scaling • Surface of concrete becomes uneven, and more water can permeate in the cracks, expand in winter, and cause more damage

NAME	NATURE	FEATURES
Damaged sealant	Related to poor maintenance, poor construction, improper design	The pre-formed sealant ages, it deteriorates, and it detaches from the reservoir's walls

CAUSES	CONSEQUENCES
• Natural aging of the sealant • Inadequate reservoir design causing the sealant to detach when joint is in maximum contraction • Accelerated aging of low-quality sealant	• Water may penetrate in the joint causing weakening of the ground (loss of bearing capacity) • Incompressible material (sand) may penetrate in the joint in the winter preventing it from closing back in the summer, causing large compressive stresses to arise

NAME	NATURE	FEATURES
Faulting	Related to poor construction and/or design	One side of a joint sinks creating a step across a longitudinal or transversal joint

CAUSES	CONSEQUENCES
• Lack of proper load transfer efficiency across the joint	• Under repeated traffic loads the loaded portion of the joint sinks in the ground creating a step in the carriageway • Vertical periodic movements of the slab may cause pumping of water from the underlying granular materials into the pavement

NAME	NATURE	FEATURES
Longitudinal cracks	Related to poor design, poor construction, unforeseeable increase of loads	Longitudinal cracks running parallel to longitudinal joints

CAUSES	CONSEQUENCES
• Warping and curling stresses underestimated at design stage • Flexural strength and/or thickness of concrete lower than designed	• Under warping or curling stresses, the internal portions of the slab may periodically bend downwards losing contact with the support • Traffic repetitions may cause tensile stresses on the unsupported slab, causing it to break

NAME	NATURE	FEATURES	
Transversal cracks	Related to poor design, poor construction, unforeseeable increase of loads	Transversal cracks running parallel to transverse contraction joints	

CAUSES	CONSEQUENCES
• Contraction joints spacing is excessive • Delayed cutting of contraction joints • Very rigid foundation • High restraint from foundation • Unforeseeable increase of traffic loads • Flexural strength and/or thickness of concrete lower than designed	• Under warping or curling stresses, the internal portions of the slab may periodically bend downward losing contact with the support • Traffic repetitions may cause tensile stresses on the unsupported slab, causing it to break

NAME	NATURE	FEATURES	
Scaling	Poor quality of concrete	The cement paste near the surface of the concrete is progressively deteriorated and lost	

CAUSES	CONSEQUENCES
• Poor freeze-thaw resistance of concrete in presence of deicing salts • High surface absorption of concrete (high water–cement ratio, poor curing, wrong mix design)	• The surface of concrete is weakened • Potholes may form • Riding quality and safety are reduced

NAME	NATURE	FEATURES	
Spalling	Improper construction	Semi-circular chunks of concrete detach from the concrete surface across the joints	

CAUSES	CONSEQUENCES
• Misaligned dowel bars across the joint cause localized compressive stresses to arise in the concrete surrounding the bars	• Joint is weakened, sealant may be lost, water may filtrate • Potholes may form • Riding quality and safety are reduced

NAME	NATURE	FEATURES
Polished surface	Improper quality of concrete	The surface of the pavement appears smooth, aggregates are visible, and appear polished

CAUSES	CONSEQUENCES
• Use of low-strength aggregates that can quickly polish under traffic • Inadequate mix design (segregating mix) • Improper texturing of the concrete surface when it was placed	• Loss of skid resistance • Riding safety is reduced

Recommended Reading

Books

- Alexander, M. and S. Mindess 2019. *Aggregates in Concrete.* New York: CRC Press.
- Delatte, N. 2017. *Concrete Pavement Design, Construction and Performance.* New York: CRC Press.
- Huang, Y.H. 2004. *Pavement Analysis and Design.* New Jersey: Prentice Hallr.
- Portland Cement Association (PCA). 2001. *Design and Control of Concrete Mixtures.*
- Taylor, P. 2019. *Curing Concrete.* New York: CRC Press.

Guidelines

- American Concrete Institute. 2007. ACI Education Bulletin E1-07: Aggregates for Concrete.
- American Concrete Institute. 2001. ACI 308R-01: Guide to Curing Concrete.
- American Concrete Pavement Association. 2018. ACPA Technical Bulletin: Concrete Pavement Joint Sealing/Filling.
- Federal Highway Administration. 2019. FHWA-HIF-18-012: Specifying, Designing, and Proportioning Paving Concrete
- Federal Highway Administration. 2006. FHWA-HRT-06-117: Freeze-Thaw Resistance of Concrete with Marginal Air Content
- Federal Highway Administration. 1996. FHWA HI-96-027: Construction of Portland Cement Concrete Pavements
- Federal Highway Administration. 2019. *Technical Advisory: Concrete Pavement Joints.* https://www.coursehero.com/file/70735980/FHWA-Concrete-Pavements-Jointspdf.
- Government of the United States, Department of Defense. 2019. Proportioning Concrete Mixtures with Graded Aggregates for Rigid Airfield Pavements. *Tri-Service Pavements Working Group Manual.*

Papers

- Burke, M.P., Jr. 2004. Reducing Bridge Damage Caused by Pavement Forces Part 1: Some Examples.
- Burke, M.P. Jr. 2004. Reducing Bridge Damage Caused by Pavement Forces Part 2: The Phenomenon.
- Hansen, W. et al. 2000. Evaluation of Freeze-Thaw Durability of Concrete Pavements with Excellent Long-Term Performance. *Concrete Science and Engineering.* RILEM Publications SARL.
- Shilstone. 1990. Concrete Mixture Optimization. In *Concrete International.* July.
- Mack, J.W. 1993. Isolation and Expansion Joints in Concrete Pavements. *Concrete Construction.* 1 September.

Standards

- ASTM International. 2003. *ASTM C33: Standard Specification for Concrete Aggregates.*
- Building and Construction Authority (BCA). 2008. *EN 12620: Aggregates for Concrete - A New Approach to Specifying Aggregates.*
- British Standard. 2001. *EN 206-1: Concrete Specification, Production and Conformity.*

Bibliography

American Concrete Institute (ACI). 2013. *ACI Concrete Terminology*. Michigan: ACI. https://www.concrete.org/portals/0/files/pdf/ACI_Concrete_Terminology.pdf.

ASTM International. 2021. ASTM C78 Standard Test Method for Flexural Strength of Concrete (Using Simple Beam with Third-Point Loading). https://www.astm.org/c0078_c0078m-21.html.

ASTM International. 2020a. ASTM C131 Standard Test Method for Resistance to Degradation of Small-Size Coarse Aggregate by Abrasion and Impact in the Los Angeles Machine. https://www.astm.org/c0131_c0131m-20.html.

ASTM International. 2020b. ASTM C143 Standard Test Method for Slump of Hydraulic-Cement Concrete. https://www.astm.org/c0143_c0143m-20.html.

ASTM International. 2019. ASTM C556 Standard Test Method for Total Evaporable Moisture Content of Aggregate by Drying. https://www.astm.org/c0566-19.html.

ASTM International. 2018a. ASTM C33 Standard Specification for Concrete Aggregates. https://www.astm.org/c0033_c0033m-18.html.

ASTM International. 2018b. ASTM D4944 Standard Test Method for Field Determination of Water (Moisture) Content of Soil by the Calcium Carbide Gas Pressure Tester. https://www.astm.org/d4944-18.html.

ASTM International. 2017a. ASTM C403 Standard Test Method for Time of Setting of Concrete Mixtures by Penetration Resistance. https://www.astm.org/c0403_c0403m-16.html.

ASTM International. 2017b. ASTM C494 Standard Specification for Chemical Admixtures for Concrete. https://www.astm.org/c0494_c0494m-05.html.

ASTM International. 2017c. ASTM D5731 Standard Test Method for Determination of the Point Load Strength Index of Rock and Application to Rock Strength Classifications. https://www.astm.org/d5731-16.html.

ASTM International. 2010. ASTM C260 Standard Specification for Air-Entraining Admixtures for Concrete. https://www.astm.org/c0260-06.html.

ASTM International. n.d. ASTM C138 Standard Test Method for Density (Unit Weight), Yield, and Air Content (Gravimetric) of Concrete -- eLearning Course. https://www.astm.org/astm-tpt-192.html.

Bamforth, P. 2018. *Control of cracking caused by restrained deformation in concrete* (C766). Ciria. https://www.ciria.org/ItemDetail?iProductCode=C766&Category=BOOK&WebsiteKey=3f18c87a-d62b-4eca-8ef4-9b09309c1c91.

Bell, F.G. 2007. *Engineering Geology.* UK: Elsevier. https://www.academia.edu/9448940/Engineering_Geology_Second_Edition_By_F_G_Bell.

Bradbury, R. D., 1938. *Reinforced Concrete Pavements.* Washington, D.C.: Wire Reinforcement Institute.

Burke, M.P. Jr. 2004. Reducing Bridge Damage Caused by Pavement Forces Part 1: Some Examples. *Concrete International.* Vol.26 (1). Michigan: ACI. https://trid.trb.org/view/686379.

Burke, M.P. Jr. 2004. Reducing Bridge Damage Caused by Pavement Forces Part 2: The Phenomenon. Concrete International. Vol.26 (2). Michigan: ACI. https://trid.trb.org/view/689565.

Delatte, N. 2014. *Concrete Pavement Design, Construction, and Performance.* Boca Raton: CRC Press. https://www.taylorfrancis.com/books/mono/10.1201/b17043/concrete-pavement-design-construction-performance-norbert-delatte.

British Standards Institution. 2021. BS EN 206:2013+A2:2021: Concrete. Specification, Performance, Production and Conformity. https://shop.bsigroup.com/products/concrete-specification-performance-production-and-conformity-2/standard.

British Standards Institution. 2020. BS EN 1097-2: Tests for Mechanical and Physical Properties of Aggregates - Part 2: Methods for the determination of resistance to fragmentation. https://shop.bsigroup.com/products/tests-for-mechanical-and-physical-propertiesof-aggregates-methods-for-the-determination-of-resistance-to-fragmentation-1/tracked-changes.

British Standards Institution. 2019a. BS EN 12350-2: Testing Fresh Concrete. Slump test. https://shop.bsigroup.com/products/testing-fresh-concreteslump-test-2/tracked-changes.

British Standards Institution. 2019b. BS EN 12350-6: Testing Fresh Concrete. Density. https://shop.bsigroup.com/products/testing-fresh-concretedensity-2/tracked-changes.

British Standards Institution. 2002. BS EN 12620: Aggregates for Concrete. https://shop.bsigroup.com/products/aggregates-for-concrete/standard.

Federal Highway Administration. 2019. *Technical Advisory: Concrete Pavement Joints.* https://www.coursehero.com/file/70735980/FHWA-Concrete-Pavements-Jointspdf.

Huang, Y.H. 2004. *Pavement Analysis and Design.* New Jersey: Prentice Hallr.

International Society for Rock Mechanics, Commission on Testing Methods. 1985. Suggested Method for Determining Point Load Strength. *International Journal of Rock Mechanics and Mining Sciences & Geomechanics Abstracts.* Vol. 22 (2). Great Britain: Pergamon Press. https://www.sciencedirect.com/science/article/abs/pii/0148906285923277.

Mack, J.W. 1993. Isolation and Expansion Joints in Concrete Pavements. *Concrete Construction.* 1 September.

Mehta, P.K and J.M. Monteiro. 2005. *Concrete: Microstructure, Properties, and Materials.* https://www.semanticscholar.org/paper/Concrete%3A-Microstructure%2C-Properties%2C-and-Materials-Mehta-Monteiro/a708f7c9bac26de7317646e0c78152a869785ba8.

Newman, J. and B.S. Choo, eds. 2003. *Advanced Concrete Technology.* UK: Elsevier.

NRMCA (1992). https://www.countymaterials.com/en/downloads/industry-tech-documents/concrete-in-practice-cips#gsc.tab=0.

Taylor, P. 2019. *Curing Concrete.* NY: CRC Press.

Walraven, J.C. et al. Theory and Experiments on the Mechanical Behavior of Cracks in Plain and Reinforced Concrete Subjected to Shear Loading. https://repository.tudelft.nl/islandora/object/uuid%3A3d68bd1a-465d-4590-b33c-7ede99bbc251.